regime 01

a magazine of new writing

regime
books

Regime 01 Edited by Peter Jeffery OAM, Nathan Hondros, Damon Lockwood and Chris Palazzolo.

Published by Regime Books in Australia, 2012.
First Floor, 456 William Street, Perth.
www.regimebooks.com.au
www.twitter.com/nathanhondros

Cover image of Mars courtesy of NASA/JPL-Caltech/Cornell/Arizona State Univ.

ISBN 978-0-646-58284-9
ISSN 2200-7822

CONTENTS

Andrew Burke

Notebook 'singing they sang'

singing they sang
one, two…then paused
only to sing the count in rhythm
one, two, three, four
          feet stomping the floor
                    give peace a chance
                    give peace a chance
I remember before them
listening to Tom Paxton
singing he sang
                    peace in the world
                    or the world in pieces
pointing his plectrum at
all fascists

~

then there was the local man
who put a cassette machine
into the polished trunk of a tree –
          he didn't hear the tree
                    singing
                    a different suite song
          for every season…

a dove in a she-oak
          listens as I write
a small sparrow
          chirps and chitters
in a red nut bush –

text in the context
song from the nest

~

on the road to Gundagai
cows lunch by
the rest area...

riding a Greyhound bus
thinking of Kerouac and co
in this sparse
Australian landscape on
an air-conditioned coach
reading AA recovery stories
socking water back

writing now with
a Tasmanian Poetry Festival pen
chitter-chatter from
Chinese girls behind me

transcendental clouds
differ day to day
they sit above
gentle hillocks
like meditating sheep

~

small timber cottage
among ancestors
untrimmed

old man at the gate
likewise

~

leaf green differs
as
seasons move on

Vivaldi's four seasons
not native here

here they count six
      in this land full
            of extremes
deserts and flood plains
snow falls and droughts

you can't
change a land's character
with nomenclature

~

           sitting in
the swill lounge
of the BP Roadstop
in North Albury

           thinking of
blackbirds sitting atop
shorn sheep in
cropped paddocks

           seeing a
tandem Reflex transport truck
with Recycle logos and

enough paper
to confetti the capital

here we are
in the abused landscape
of Gondwanaland
thinking
      how many poems
           could fit on
    that!

recycled ideas of
      the Great Canon
a tolerable reflex

Virginia Jealous

Oiling the Decks

Eyre Telegraph Station

Scrimshaw dunes rise behind
this house, their etched paths carved
by feet, recurved by wind
then smoothed by scudding sand
to matte ivory. Souvenirs of sea
surround the verandah, textured
like sandpaper and thirsty
for oil: while lifting crumbling
whalebones the heavy embrace
of a bleached rib's graceful curve
flenses mine, leaving traces
inked on skin by bone.

Amanda Joy

Conjoined

*'…decay is not simply a middle term
between the grain and the ear of wheat.'*
                    George Bataille

Chinese New Year in a room
with little room, not enough
to dance, there are no chairs
Nowhere to sit. A man telling
us he is a dragon.

An algorithm with too many steps
becomes hard to follow, instructs –

Go down to the forest, with its absence
of human dimensions, until
you get there. Consider –

The spectral evidence.
Having been seen on the other side
of town cursing a cow
while you were asleep
in your bed.

The child afraid of the dark, given
a beautiful name impossible
to fill Sits in a doorway watching
two lines of traffic heading in two
opposite directions.

The other child, papillionate
butterflied at the chest, cries out,
vibrates on a page without pain
or colour.

Ari Mattes

The Toys Do Not Speak

Some of Dr Fielding's earliest daydreams were about death. As a five or six year old he would imagine being crushed under the front wheel of his papa's four wheel drive; at ten he was jumping in front of the train on his way to school, nebulising into red mist. In his teenage years he would fantasise about turning the wheel of his Holden HQ an inch or so to the right, crashing into the oncoming traffic at a hundred Ks an hour.

Now that he was actually dying, he wanted to savour every moment up to the point at which he would start kicking and floundering and clawing at the rope. He could see, in the wardrobe mirror, the blood rushing to his head, the circle of white around the rope as it cut into his neck.

The pressure of asphyxiation, though, was comforting, rather than oppressive, a warmth of sensation belying the gruesome descriptions of hanging about which he'd read in suicide blogs. He closed his eyes, tried to evacuate his mind of all thought. A mallet beat its systolic tattoo against the inside of his chest, counterpointing the more ambient noise of the rain outside. He opened his eyes and inhaled deeply. The smell of jasmine suited the dusky light filtering in through the window; the drone of invisible cicadas. He'd never have to tend to the garden again. It would grow wild – let Sarah worry about it.

The act of dying would bring one to the limit of knowledge, he used to tell Sarah. He prayed he would remain conscious long enough, now, to mentally modulate the kind of epiphany he was certain would come somewhere during the final act.

I

He finished his lecture thus: 'And that, my dear friends, marked not only the end of the Mariner, but the Albatross too.' And with a sweeping, inevitable logic his students began talking, packing their bags, filing out of the lecture theatre. He sighed, wishing he could shut his eyes and dis-envision the brown panelling and fluorescent light that characterised every work day.

He was a little sad at the end of each lecture. He'd been carrying a mountain for the past two hours; speaking eloquently within and against the imaginary universe he'd created for himself and his students. A gun, shooting out ideas and then interpreting them with a dexterity simplicity clarity that astonished even himself.

Then it was over; the world would shrivel up and he'd become, once again, a stone in a pointless prune, waiting for something to happen. It would have been more climactic – more palatable – if there'd been applause at the finish. His goal, through ten years as a mediocre academic at a mediocre university, had been to deliver a lecture, just once, that culminated in applause. His students would stand up, characters from one of those sentimental films of the fifties, Mr Chips or something.

But you were never applauded; you never had students asking anything other than the most pragmatic questions (assignment dates; word limits) and you never felt you were contributing anything more substantial to the world than the conditioning of a plague of perpetually precocious, and perpetually ignorant, rats.

He loaded his tan briefcase, reset the AV equipment. The next lecturer was hovering around. They never spoke – they'd look away as they swapped positions, as though each was aware of some obscure crime on the part of the other.

'Excuse me,' the next lecturer said. Fielding turned back from the door. 'Someone's left their phone.'

Their bloody phones! How many times had he been distracted mid-sentence by the vision of a student tucked over his or her fluorescent toy. He told them to switch off their phones at the beginning of every lecture, but they'd just look at him and smile, barely trying to hide their impudence. It was under Sofia's seat. Sofia – his brightest student; his best looking, with that tight, tanned skin, skin that'd stretch the perfect amount before snapping back into place.

He grunted his thanks to the lecturer and stuffed the phone into his briefcase. He exited the lecture theatre, leaving the brown vinyl foldtop desks and tiers of empty seats to the next batch of students. He wondered if Sarah would be making dinner tonight or if he should drop by the supermarket and pick something up.

II

Dr Fielding was sitting in his armchair, a pile of essays beside him. Sarah was on the couch opposite, eyes dull and glued to an American cop show.

Exhausted, as usual, after a twelve-hour shift at the hospital.

He picked up an essay. 'P' was pencilled on its cover sheet, not for pass, but for plagiarism. This was the aspect of grading essays he found most exhilarating – checking the passages he'd marked with an asterisk against google scholar. The transitions from students' bumbling prose to the sharply analytical writing of plagiarised scholars were always glaringly obvious. If his search was successful, as they usually were, he could suspend, for a minute, his pastoral role as an educator, and let rip with vitriolic comments: 'a waste of my time,' 'shameless behaviour', 'pathetic'. Their faces would shrivel up as he returned their papers; the tears well in their pleading eyes. He'd make sure the plagiarism charges stuck; he'd make sure they passed through the dean's office and stuck, like little pieces of used gum, to their academic records.

'Stephen…' Sarah's voice broke him from his reverie. 'Stephen – why did you change your ring tone?'

He turned from his laptop, puzzled. He hadn't changed his ring tone: but there it was, a pop tune clanging from his briefcase.

'I didn't, honey,' he said, then smiled, remembering. 'I picked up a student's phone after class. Forgot to hand it in.'

'That's odd,' said his wife. 'Would you like me to answer it?'

Stephen blushed. What a horrible idea – the news would spread around the class room faster than gossip around a small town. What did she sound like? his students would ask one another. Old?

'No,' he said – Sarah's eyes narrowed, suspicious – 'Don't worry about it. I'll give it to her tomorrow.'

'At least switch it off or something. It's annoying.'

He returned to his laptop – a clear sign there was no need for further discussion. He watched his wife, in his peripheral vision; she leant back into the couch and focused once again on the flickering screen. He glanced at the tele. A loud advert for a spaceman action figure came on. 'Attention: The Toys Do Not Speak' flashed, fluoro yellow, across the bottom of the screen.

The words flashed into his mind that night as he lay next to his sleeping wife. The toys do not speak.

III

That thought led to another, and sometime after two am he found himself back in his armchair, Sofia's phone in his hands. He would return it tomorrow…

He wondered if she was popular. If she was dating any of her classmates. The thought excited him – the idea that a hook up had been initiated against the soundtrack of his lectures. He scrolled through Sofia's contact list. Georgia – she was the redhead who usually sat with Sofia. Were they close friends, or casual colleagues? He opened the contact: no recent activity between them. Obviously not very close. Unless they saw each other so often, like best friends (lovers?) that there was no need for them to text one another.

He could start the conversation. He could write anything – organise a meeting; write something cryptic, sweet, invent a name – 'Missed you after class today, Babe. Pinky was XOXO – HILARIOUS!'

The grandfather clock ticked on towards three as he considered the possibilities. He could see his silhouette full and gloomy in the glass across the dial. He moved his head from side to side, but the silhouette failed to respond.

He could call her a slag, warn her to keep away from Pinky (was that even a real name?). He could tell her he (she'd think 'she') loved her – that he (she) wanted to feel the ripeness of her breasts in his (her) mouth. *That* would change the dynamic in tomorrow's lecture! Of course, he could replace the phone in his briefcase and hand it in to the office.

To text, or not to text? Life had become exquisitely simple, and Fielding was thrilled by the clarity of the proposition. For once it wasn't just a matter of philosophy; his actions would affect the lives of real people in a concrete way. But, somehow, to toss a coin seemed trite, beneath his poetic nature. So how to decide, and to respect unfalteringly, the outcome of the decision? His marking sheet was on the coffee table beside him. He picked it up, laid it on his lap. He could close his eyes, rotate the foolscap paper a number of times, place his finger on it…If he landed on a mark higher than seventy he would send a text, lower he would replace the phone in his briefcase and think nothing more of it. Distinction or above: sms; credit or below: no sms.

He landed on Whitney Barringer and sighed with relief – he'd given her seventy-eight, a distinction, for her last essay. He had no doubt at all that everything up to this point in his life had conspired to produce this result. That the gods were, indeed, on his side.

IV

The next morning, Sarah pointed at the phone on the kitchen table. 'Looks like you got a message,' she said.

Fielding had texted Georgia, had commented on the luscious red hair between her legs; he wanted to pluck it out with his teeth. He'd enjoyed it so much he'd scrolled through the rest of Sofia's contacts, sending every female random, mostly obscene, texts, signing off every message as 'Papa Fuck'.

He picked up the phone. Sarah grabbed his wrist. 'I was kidding,' she said. 'You can't look at that.'

'Of course not, honey.' He smiled and made a gun with his fingers. 'Gotcha.'

'You're a worry, Stephen Fielding.' She turned back to her grapefruit and newspaper.

It was a painful twenty minutes for Fielding. The muesli tasted blander than usual and Sarah's freshly squeezed OJ was sour. Maybe she'd over-chomp on the grapefruit and her teeth would burst through the bottom of her chin. Maybe the grapefruit was a hand grenade, and he'd spend the afternoon picking the shrapnel and bone out of the cream walls (he'd wanted to paint them apricot; she found bright colours too stressful) and cleaning away the blood with soap and warm water.

Finally she dumped her dishes in the sink, gathered up her belongings, kissed him on the forehead. 'I'll be home late tonight,' she said. 'I have to work on a paper for the conference. Teenage depression and borderline personality disorders. Yuck!'

He had the phone in his hand before she'd shut the door.

'Dear Papa Fuck,' he read, 'Sofia told me she lost her phone, so I take it you're some kind of lusty perv dreaming about us lassies menstruating and smearing our fecal matter all over your face. But that's okay. I'm a lusty perv too. I wanna meet, Papa. I'll be at Unicaf on Central Boulevarde between eight and ten tonight. You'll know who I am. I won't be wearing any panties and you'll be able to smell my cunt. Love, Ms Slut.'

V

There was every reason in the world not to go. Stephen made a list of them as he sat in his office. It might be a set up – Ms Slut was probably in league with Sofia, running some kind of sting to see who'd nicked her phone. They'd be waiting with police. Or their aim could be rudimentary humiliation. They'd have a camera and post the footage on Blackboard for the rest of the students and faculty to see. Or they'd threaten to show the messages to Sarah unless he gave them high marks, money. The most likely scenario, obviously, was that no one would show up.

There was every reason in the world not to go, and Dr Fielding had convinced himself there was no way in the world that he would, when a whiff of perfume from one of his colleagues drifted in under the door. It was floral, jasmine, and reminded Fielding of primary school. Its semaphore was clear: fuck it – go anyway.

The café was surprisingly crowded for a Wednesday night. Groups of prim students in collegiate clothing were sitting around tables discussing,

Fielding supposed, the latest pop songs, the latest digital technology. He remembered a time not too long ago when students were still shaggy haired, grungy ratbags who never shut up about radical politics and philosophy. Now he was the grungy ratbag, the dinosaur in the shabby suit. He ordered a latte, sat in a corner with a view of door. It was seven thirty – he'd be able to observe everyone who came and went.

But by eight forty-five the crowd was thinning out, and he hadn't noticed any eligible customers. One girl had given him what he'd thought was a knowing look, but had then gone off with a slick-looking jock.

'Papa?' He jerked around. Standing to his right she was; she was probably in her early twenties. She had very pale skin, short jet black hair – not a bad body, though perhaps a little thick around the hips. She removed her backpack (were there patches sewed on it?), sat in the chair opposite Fielding.

Fielding swallowed, knew he was blushing. 'Hello,' he said.

Her pale blue eyes darted over him. She was wearing an inordinate amount of eyeliner – odd, given she had on thick black-rimmed glasses. She had a sprinkle of freckles across her nose which immediately reminded Fielding of an illustrated rabbit. She was undeniably cute.

She smiled – her tongue poked out, an accident. 'Hi,' she said. 'You got my message…'

The idea lingered between them uncomfortably. Stephen hadn't admitted anything yet. He could still feign ignorance, assert that there'd been some kind of hideous misunderstanding.

He shifted about in his chair. 'Your name – it's Veronica?'

'Yep.' Her voice was pretty.

'Like Archie,' he said.

'Sorry?'

'Archie – the comic. Betty and Veronica.'

She looked bewildered. 'Sorry – before my time, I guess.'

He blushed again. He felt uncomfortably old interacting with students under even the most ordinary of circumstances.

She leaned forward, winked at him, self-possessed. 'I knew you weren't going to be a psycho. I could tell from your message you were just pretending.'

He smiled. 'How do you know I'm not?'

She shrugged. 'I know people. I know people first time I look at 'em. You're not a psycho – a little introverted, sure, and bored – and, I'm guessing, unhappy – but not a psycho.'

'And,' he leaned forward, 'how do I know that you're not a "psycho"?'

She splayed her skirt down between her legs. 'I guess there's one way to find out.'

He thought he was going to be sick. How could he meet her on equal terms, mould his face into as brazen a mask as hers? Should he stand up, walk away, and then turn back at the door – say, 'let's go', or something?

She was laughing. But there was no malice in her voice. 'Don't worry,' she said. 'Let's have a coffee, eh, and see how it goes from there?'

It went pretty damn well. Papa Fuck stumbled over his words at first, potholes on an unknown road; but Ms Slut filled them in for him and guided him with a gentle and willing arm. Soon Papa Fuck was making Ms Slut laugh with anecdotes stolen from books of the past, books he knew most people had never read. And she was looking at him with eyes that reflected respect and wonder and awe at his intelligence, his humour, his verbal prowess. Soon Papa Fuck and Ms Slut were locking arms, and stumbling around the night, drunk on each other's ideas of good conversation as they found a taxi, and then a motel, and then a room.

And Papa Fuck called out his wife's name as he climaxed, not for his or Ms Slut's benefit, but to draw the name of her face across the stars, to piss on it. He sprayed white blood over the face that had ruined his career, the face that had sapped the life from him, the face that had forced him to marry too young by falling pregnant and then duped him through miscarriage, flushing womb and flesh into the obscene sewers of unwritten, personal history. That night he dreamed the face's vagina was a swamp, and that he was a mosquito trapped within it, and woke up knowing that nothing was a matter of chance.

VI

At first it was thrilling – it reminded Fielding of that clandestine joy of being a kid and sneaking a slice of cold pizza in the middle of the night, of having a gulp of milk straight from the carton. Years of frustration with a wife who made decisions for him without noticing she was doing so, who referred to him as part of a 'we' everytime she spoke to her pilates-loving friends ('*we* enjoyed that play'; '*we* don't like Hawaii – it's too touristy') – who was simply the most visible symptom in the disorder of his life – became null and void care of this quirky and perverse girl, materialised before him, it seemed, as an antidote to reality.

Veronica had a way of looking at things that was entirely new to him – that resurrected his faith in chance. One night on King Street (they'd been to a movie) a tramp asked him for money. Fielding reached for his wallet but Ronnie stayed his hand. 'He doesn't need money,' she said. She set herself square in front of the hobo, and yanked up her T-shirt. 'Beats five bucks,' she said, openly sneering. She seemed to be completely without inhibition – and it wasn't just that she was young and reckless.

Their sex – he'd called it love-making, once, and she'd stuck her fingers in her mouth and pretended to gag – was spontaneous, as filthy as he'd imagined it could be. Suicide sex, she called it. They'd have sex two, three times in a night, and twice again in the morning, and he'd go and lecture and not give a damn about the kids and their phones and their open, smiling contempt.

But alas, the cliché that familiarity breeds contempt (Fielding winced when he read stuff like that) proved, like most clichés, maddeningly true. He started to notice defects in her that at first he'd been willing to overlook. She used dental floss after everything she ate, for example; even if it was just a bite of an apple, she'd reach for her endless supply of floss and he'd have to sit and listen to the sound of the tape rubbing back and forth across her teeth for five minutes, the sound of the tape as it cut into her gums.

An annoying habit he could tolerate, but ignorance and lack of perception were other matters. For the first few months he'd found it endearing that she failed to comprehend most of his cultural references, even to events of very recent periods – it made him feel comfortably avuncular. But when he had to explain television shows and movies from the 1980s – when he had to clarify that Magnum wasn't only a type of ice cream…

And she would ask him questions about Sarah. Cute at first, too, her peformance as 'jealous mistress.' But the questions became increasingly probing and she started to coerce awkward comparisons with herself (what face did Sarah make when she came? what was her pussy like – waxed or bushy?). He did his best to reassure her – she was young and sexy, his wife old and sexless (she was only in her late thirties, for Christ's sake!) – but it started to feel too much like work. And now he'd stay behind at his office and do research for real; he'd lie to both Sarah and Ronnie and go off on his own, maybe get an ice cream in Manly or something, enjoy his solitude amongst the twilit crowds.

He realised, one night after they'd screwed, that no choice remained but to end the affair – the random spontaneity of their relationship had disappeared. He was sitting on her bed checking his e-mails; she was trying to distract him, pawing at him like an over-indulged puppy.

'So,' she said. 'You coming to Metraxas tomorrow night?' Metraxas was a new club in King's Cross. He shut his laptop.

'It's Friday night. I couldn't possibly come up with a suitable excuse for Sarah.'

'You stayed here Friday *and* Saturday a couple of weeks ago.'

'Yes – but, like I told you then, dolly dearest, my delightful wife was on one of her yoga retreats.'

'You promised.' She flashed him doe eyes, her best pouty face.

'I said I'd go – *sometime*. I never promised it'd be this weekend.'

'But that's what you always say. You won't do it because it's something I want to do, not something you've organised. You only ever call me when you feel like it.'

He chuckled bitterly. '*Of course* I only ever call you when I feel like it. Why would I call you otherwise? I wouldn't call anyone if I didn't feel like talking to them. Or have something important to say.'

Her face relaxed into a smile. She kissed his neck. 'I'm sorry,' she said. 'I'm beginning to sound like your wife. I know. I just get so lonely, waiting around for you all the time, Papa.'

But no matter how much she tried to make it seem light or like a joke, he was unable to ignore the feeling of panic rising in his throat. He began dressing.

'Going already?' she said. There it was again.

'I have to get home. Sarah will be wondering where I am.'

'Okay Papa. But come see me again soon, hey? A couple of dicks a week aren't enough…' She spread her legs, pulled her nightie down, coy as a teenage whore.

'Sure,' he said. 'Maybe we can go to that club next Friday. I think Sarah has a conference on.'

'Sure,' she said. He blew her a kiss at the door, dreading the equally painful conversation he was sure was to come with his wife. Having to lie to your mistress, having to lie to your wife…Perhaps in reality exciting vignettes always turned into dreary sagas.

They struggled on for a month or so longer. Ronnie hurled a string of insults at him when he broke it off, then tried to woo him back via his pants, and then insulted him some more when that didn't work. But she was young, she would be fine. It was Sarah he was worried about. Sarah – oblivious with her own work, unwilling or unable to admit there was perfection and imperfection in anything else. That nice things could smell rotten, and that rotten things could taste nice. Still she had no idea, still she didn't know what real shame and disgrace felt like.

VII

Fielding opened the dining room cabinet and rummaged behind a pile of seldom used tablecloths. He found what he was after – a dirty movie he'd made with Veronica, burned onto DVD. He'd watched it a few times before stashing it away, none too carefully, for a rainy day.

Well, today it was raining. Today it was raining, and Sarah would be annoyed. Sarah had expected him to bring in the washing and now it was soaked and would stink. He stood at the back door, watching the rain splash into puddles and onto the bottoms of his trousers. He liked the city when it rained – it was the only time it smelled fresh, earthy. He closed the door, retrieved the rope, still wrapped in plastic, from the storage space under the stairs. He scrawled 'S.' on a scrap of paper, placed it on his wife's side of the bed next to the DVD.

He hoped he'd timed it correctly. When he'd googled 'length of time – die hanging' he'd found a blog that said, given his weight (eighty-four kilos) and age (forty-two), it should take about half an hour. Provided he didn't snap his neck with a lengthy fall. It was five fifteen. Sarah was due home at six, as he'd promised to take her to dinner and a movie.

He set the stool in the study – it was only a couple of feet from the ground – and attached the rope to the chandelier fixture. He placed the noose around his neck, pulling it tight. This was how a novice acrobat felt, he thought, climbing the ladder to his first trapeze. For some reason he remembered Yeats' 'The Circus Animals' Desertion'.

He smiled inside for the first time in a long time. His dream of a self-conceived and interpreted death was coming to fruition – the first and last sidereal adventure in a life lived on the footpath. Perhaps, Fielding thought as he knocked over the stool, the toys did speak after all.

Barnaby Smith

Autopsy (Song for the CBD)

On a precarious perch,
virtuoso urban drumpoets
are standing arms aloft with rage.

They are riding buses and brushing their teeth with rage.
They are making nests of lighters and shards,
they are buzzards over windmills,
raging at this corporeal befuddle of gonococcic pains.

Go see for yourself, using the scalpel,
the haunted inner space of the mottled
and flecked stallions of the street,
working in tandem on gratuitous alchemy
in this breathtaking laboratory.
I have not moved well with the times.

Revolution is a small town, and a child's name.
An exulted barbarian community
where the locals aren't people,
and the people aren't local.
The governor an earnest black rooster
with rosy cheeks
and a fancy for the Himalayas and high heels.

There are plastic stone circles
using the sun to measure those contemptible dreams;
those infidelity dances raising the spirits
of the shackled legions who have gone before.
They tell me their rhythm has died,
And ask me finally, to take to the floor.

Matt Davies

Fifty Dollars a Dance

The bitumen lingering longer than slower with
No moon to croon on the fallacies in darkness.
A red neon transmit one to the USA, but there's
No need. Coffee and cigarettes are mere steps
Away. It's 4am and the store's flowers are rotten
You want them anyway to dispel the sheen of
Unnatural cleanliness and IKEA accessory order.
You want living colour to settle your sight upon,
To fade with something transitory, to whip a soul.

Until you pass a Cetaphil-soft skinned hooker
In the context of the indistinct. A serious beret,
A gentle tan, shivering under the dilapidated shop
Where tradition dictates they stand. A polite, 'How
You doing?' startles me none, but the sight of this
Woman flowers me in concupiscence. But modest
And refined. Fifty-dollars a dance if I could take her
There, through my unremembered eras, dispelling
Notions of the forthcoming act with a debonair stare.

Adrian Flavell

peak-hour

crowds

stretch the street

like a sheet
on a new-made bed

Petri Ivalo Sinda

The Sound of Biological Functions

Life is behind the times, only death strives to be punctual, and disease is always early. Try to resist this, refute this, and problems pile up like fruit eager to spoil.

Daylight awakens streaks of joy in me; joy in the streaks of dawn cirrus clouds that is, so tight and sharp at their leading edges before they feather out. God's own calligraphy lessons. (Nice penmanship.)

I was tight and sharp once.

I sit facing the open curtains. At first the afterimage of sunrise seems to glower before my eyes for half a day, perfusing golden heat into my cheeks' subcutaneous layers. Later, with heat saturation, there's some kind of switchover in my head and time swerves, warps ahead at a faster rate. From then, it seems every sunrise is indistinguishable from sunset, periods of daylight sweeping over and over me like a pell mell lighthouse beam. All round, the landscape beats to the rhythmic surge and release of so many bright hours a day, tides of light in snappy ebb and flow. Between dawn to the time the curtains are whisked shut at dusk, the windows discharge cumulative pulses of light – *booms* of light. The sun's gigantic heartbeat. Is it any wonder my eyelids become diaphragms of warmth pulsing in time to the sun's heartbeat? Only through my eyelids' red pulsing do I remain connected to the world.

Ah, not quite; my bones also enjoy soaking up all the heat they can. I have to put up with hot and cold flushes all the time, chills and fevers racing over my skin in time to the lighthouse sweeps of daylight. It's poor form for a man to complain, but in truth I wish they would let me stay outside longer. There, the warmth loiters close by. Cherish the dawn. Cherish everything, while you're at it.

I'm itching to be out in the courtyard now, but the missus is still busy with domestics. Mustn't complain. Someone has to go first. My time will find its mark.

The great outdoors has the pace I like, though. Television programs? Too fast, too choppy; all breakneck edits and jump cuts – just like pornography, actually. Get me outside where I can revel in the ecstasy of vibrating air, follow grass growing and peruse flowers opening like footage of prickly bubbles popping. Most times the missus rightly divines my needs and wheels me outside, leaves me there. She's learnt to read me. Just now, in fact, she spots something in the quashed language of my posture and pauses at the dishes long enough to unclip my high wheel lock and guide me out into the courtyard and set the anti-tip casters before clapping a wide brim hat onto my head for good measure. Then, impatient to address her domestics, she grants me the heartfelt benediction of her palm against my cheek as she rushes off, only it's too brief to leave behind any lasting touch. No tingling message between skins. No body memory to cherish anew. All the same, I'm pathetically grateful. Most of the time she looks after me rather than spends time with me.

Perhaps she's frightened.

Today the sunlight deposits itself so thick and fast it cements itself to the courtyard in blinding lamina. Out here all sky and light hammers me. Every now and then headaches like pressed steel stack up in my skull (though not as shrill as the *accelerando* headaches television gives me). Not that I would quit the outdoors for anything.

The capillaries under my cheeks swell with accumulated light, flaring right back up into my eyes. Great. I'll be squinting so much people will think I'm a lapsed Botox junkie.

Squinting, I keep an eye on a butterfly tediously bunting its way through midair. It leaves gentle dust whorls curling in its wake, as if shedding frail afterimages of itself.

Come suppertime o'clock, I'm wheeled back inside and installed at the head of the dinner table, children deployed along both sides. Dinner is served. I ease myself through it, mindful as a stick insect hoping not to alert predators. Soon I'm submerged beneath the herky jerky chatter of the dining room, a twittering that jolts around quicker than I can follow. I've always watched with amazement the lightning dexterity with which city-folk flap their lips about. Not what I call music, exactly. I'd prefer Noisy Miners…

The kids' insensible babble is particularly hard to stomach of late. Mustn't complain, it's entirely natural. Their antics give rise to the very hum of belonging, after all. I want to champion everything they do, I truly do. It kills me how they skim past me quick as they can when dinner's over, rarely swinging by close enough for a goodnight kiss. I pray they can hear it when my heart's beating; that they believe I'm still alive inside. A moot hope, really. Quick as a flash they excuse themselves from the dinner table. In vain I try to catch my eldest's eye before he exits but he fast forwards away in multicoloured blurs.

I can tell the kids – and their visiting schoolmates – only scram from the dinner table because of their haste to mock me behind safe, closed doors. I scare them. Of course they peck at me, pillory me. Only, I can't take it – especially not coming from visiting schoolgirls disgusted by this sluggish soundless statue they find skulking in their midst. A man like a stain of indeterminate age. And my slow, hurt convalescence from their ridicule only whets their appetite.

My sons…My own children.

Another troubling element they introduce into my evenings is their sheer onrush of *speed*. Far too much excitement. No letup. It destroys my nerves; it takes me hours to draw out the stress, ease back into soft time. Even back in the day I didn't favour the surplus expenditure of emotions. My determination to brook no drama remains firm. But what can *I* do? Who lip reads a statue? Furthermore, do I now also question the missus's love simply because she isn't properly attending to my needs?

At a certain hour the missus finally does notice my expression – she clamps down on the unholy terrors running around the house and marches them off to bed. Only then do I feel it's safe to try and rise and move about on my own.

Rash of me – the streak blurred movements of their little bodies have left behind searing bright copies of their motions, solid trails of afterimages that track everywhere through the house so that I fear to bump into them in case one of them recrosses his path at just that moment. I have to wait, unknit the entire cat's cradle of light, skintone and hair colour before I can once again trust myself to free and easy movement throughout the house.

Lately, it's taking longer and longer to dissolve these fossil strands of time. Like tonight, for instance. Time has metastasized into solid colours. The effect spreads: abstract chunks of motion break off from the world's continuity and jerk past like speeding cars glimpsed out the corners of the eye. The effect spreads beyond the solid colour trails to random segments of the walls, the carpets, the cupboards, doors, lamps, curtains – everything now fringed with rainbow oscillations. The children's energy has simply imparted too much motion to my world. Latent motion judders everything to and fro, as if behind every surface and object there's a loaded spring sensitive to the lightest pressure of my gaze. The world fidgets as one, everything just out of synch and vibrating with diffraction ghosts. Nauseating. Too much. Too much. Seasick in my own home.

There's no choice but to surrender to these dizzying partial impressions. Only they erupt towards you at breakneck speed – as frenzied and alarming as those insect quick thirtysomething bars which I shall never again visit, not while their dancefloors are flailing cauldrons of upraised limbs multiplying overhead.

No, I have to go easy. Tranquillity is my Shangri-La, my Lost World. I shuffle forward carefully, painstakingly, as if walking on coral, constantly testing my footing.

The joy of being alive certainly stimulates the five senses. Too much so. Ah yes, what I covet is peace. Rest. Serenity.

When I'm fully at peace, I listen in through my Eustachian whispering wall, listening to my blood making its rounds, the whole fluvial cadence of my bloodstream. Concentrating deeper, I can hear the sibilant whisperings of the liquids trickling through me, swerving to and fro, as well as bubbles galloping upwards from the pipes as they're gurgling monstrous secrets about my interior. But I'm nauseated by the gas diffusing through my spleen, liberating bubbling mucous; and by the saliva frothing inside my cheeks as I roil my tongue around; as well as the snapping elastic sound band as I chew food, sinews twanging over each other. Nor am I particularly fond of the changing pitch as I gulp air. Every time I swallow, my Adam's apple sounds like a stone being rubbed with Hessian.

I can't bear the silence. The distilled solitude. A magnifying glass for the soul, solitude resolves everything. Especially the motionless weight of a life unable to stand up, relegated to a bygone existence. Condemned to a living death:

Life of a Minimum Script.

The next day, all motion has been tranquillized to death. Here I sit, grounded in an arresting stillness like perpetual daybreak. A dawn that never quite arrives. The morning of infinity.

Torture, in other words. It's like sleepwalking only without ever going anywhere, or waking up for that matter. Between dawn and dusk I subsist in tender noon sleep, giving stark attention to the world. Life pretends to be passing by the window. I go along with the fiction just for the sake of form. What else can I do? But really, it's torture. Repetitive nowhere days loom large. Days so slow and blank they ache.

Yet I discover solitude resolves not only the banal but the beautiful, empty mystery of existence.

So I look. By visions within the mind I make investigations of the personal subconscious, not the given objective facts. All because this abstract plumbing and probing is preferable to trying to re-engage with what remains of my family life. I'm sick of all the snide arguing and complaints about my 'special needs'. I cannot abide to witness their degradation. So I avert myself. I turn away. I turn within. But then, what happens then?

For a start, time passes with a vengeance; so much so there's no device left that can measure the celestial distance between heartbeats.

Consciousness, however, seems to abhor a vacuum. Eventually the vast empty spaces begin to multiply, emerging from a deeper source to overtake me. Time begins to devour the future with praeternatural swiftness. I live among days of amazing speed.

*

'Suppertime o'clock': an infantile gloss upon the unsavoury conduct of my sisters and brothers-in-law holding forth at the dinner table. I cannot work out which conversation to follow. Crisscrossing voices skewer me with caustic intrigue (not only children mock). Soon my head churns with gossip; ill concealed whispers that jar on the nerves. 'Must be good, his life. The exquisite indolence of the man…' – Maureen the Business Suit. The missus isn't charging to my defence; siding, instead, with the snipers so she can vent at long last. Ah: this is why they're invited over so often. Social reinforcement for my public shaming.

So, it has come to this.

The missus brings up my perpetual lethargy. 'A right sloth, he is…sleeping's *his* big magic trick! Oh, it entertains the nippers for hours, that it does. *Such* a father he's proved to be!' Bangs the wineglass on the table. The motion carries. All say aye.

Once again I am transparent to hurt, reduced to a boy on his first day at primary school.

'I…I…' My words are trampled underfoot. The missus rattles on something about 'the bottled spider of his brain' – Maureen suggests they set it free outside.

The missus cheerfully explains: 'Oooh no, I'd just crush it underfoot.'

The muscled gong of my heart, muffled through chambers packed solid with meat. My heart an orchid slowly opening and closing its petals to the seasons of my blood. The wash of blood back and forth, the blood music as circuits re-complete themselves in a susurrus regular as the hiss of tides upon a flat beach. The oceanic pulsing of my head.

I am more fatigued than usual. I've afforded the family too much practice at wearing me down.

Once, I used to enjoy spending my days gazing out the loungeroom windows, viewing the street rather than the courtyard, keen to survey the anthropological epochs of styles passing out of fashion – people passing out of fashion, too.

It's like that film director lifelong cursed by his inimitable youthful smash hit: 'Hi, I used to be Peter Bogdanovich.' No devastation so unprecedented as self eviction. I sympathize though I'm always *unchanging*, always *me*. Dormant forever in this anaemic pink sarcophagus that needs more sunlight than it ever gets. Exiled from becoming, sentenced to *being*.

It's enough to leave you cabbageheaded.

What really drives me batshit is how it fails to do just that: I'm still here. Cognizant. Sane. Hypovolaemic and hypoventilatory, yes, but perfectly awake inside. Awake but powerless. And if you're powerless to engage, interact, nothing changes, ever. Any wonder the days reset themselves without warning? Soul quakes. Punctuated equilibrium of being.

Soul quakes aside, this era is congealing inside my bones. I am living amber, rapidly becoming an artefact; numbness congealed and mellified in memories, such as they are. Day by day, all I can do is spy on myself through the remaining keyhole of consciousness, reviewing the time I was asleep in an earlier stage of life. When? Last Tuesday, last Thursday? Ughh, last Thursday is indistinguishable from an æon. Lifetime voids of the skull.

Yet even eternity is inconstant, I find. The repetition of bygone days speeds up as consciousness loses parity with being. *Thoughts are the prey of time.*

I'm back again – time no longer streaking past like subway billboards. I've shaken loose out of the metro light continuum, back in specific time.

It hurts.

I hold my head still as the frost of a needlepoint headache begins to etch its barbs into me, icing me numb stroke by stroke. The key to holding off pain is all about holding absolutely still, not giving the nerves any sensation to report. No pain data: no pain. *The Way of the Statue.*

Holding still is harder than it may seem. Nowadays my head always spins with thoughts. It's just go go go; even the internal constellations of my heaviest thoughts are set to slow waltzing in astronomical time, gathered together by the inexorable gravitational pulling power of identity, presence, and phenomenologically ordered consciousness. All that aside, though, what's simply true is that thought is rooted in body. My brain is a tree that has sent its nerve roots right throughout me, so that my body is, in effect, an ambulatory brain. A free range brain. That's what it's meant to be. A brain planted in the rich soil of a human body. Grown brains stroll around in search of other brains. Grown brains fool around, have sex, brawl at night, fill out tax returns.

But something is weighing down my soil, becalming my body so nothing will grow. I cannot get myself to budge. To interact. To touch. I am trapped in myself. A hapless lodger without the power to get the electricity re-connected.

These are the thoughts that churn over in my head since time immemorial. *May God recycle my soil.*

Although my heaviest thoughts may coalesce slow as galaxies, I cannot truly claim I experience astronomical time. Not really. It's just the body's mirage, an awesome delusion sired by the heroic oasis of consciousness, which has been experiencing such drought conditions it's throwing out brave hallucinations of eternity moseying along besides me. No doubt meant to comfort me, but I don't take such mystical semaphore seriously. Comforting ideas are meaningless. Every eternity is an island. Billions of æons from now in the expanded universe, each galaxy will dwell in the dark alone, no other island galaxies visible in the void. Each person is just like that. I don't have the strength to hold my family close. No one wants to be stuck on an island, particularly a statue island. Fear conquers love. Everyone flees, everyone recedes into their own eternity. Really, there's practically nothing left for me to do other than keep slow dancing in the quicksand of my body.

And it's pulling me under.

But not quick enough, I fear.

*

The missus bends before me, feels my forehead.

'Tired,' I managed to eek out, an exhausting confession prompted by a dormant new fear. My neck is cluttered with sweat beads.

'Have a rest, dear' she orders, the corners of her mouth moueing in irony.

I'm worn out from resting all the time. Did I actually say that, or imagine it? I must break the ranks of insomnia.

'Just playing for time…' I josh, my tongue sprawling huge across my mouth like a roll of carpet. It feels raspy, and something impossibly dry tickles my throat. Something's wrong. The last two days have tapered right off, really disconnected themselves.

I turn my head too fast and the housebricks vibrate loose from one another then belatedly click back in a composite mirage. I take a deep swallow, close my eyes and tilt my head to the left. Loathsome musty disintegration foams up in my nostrils. I want to herk, but this atrophied ventriloquist only shakes out dummy coughs and spits.

When the coughing's over, I loll my head about on the recliner and stare outside, searching for more sunlight, finding there only the glowing square windows of another universe altogether, it seems like. The sky is all known blues at once, a canvas overpainted beyond count. Too many skies. As I look, the windows begin to pulse faster, brighter, and the dashing arc of the sun is way too hasty in the sky, its headlong crash into the ground alarming me. That's it, the day slips right past, trailing the sun in a brilliant arc of time. Then twilight yanks its cowl over me. Naught to do but lie back and contract the melancholy of dusk, revel in all this astral paralysis that reclines above me like an exhausted lover. Before long, darkness leans against me. I am called to the serious depths of sleep for the first time. No. No more. I will tolerate no more rest. I want to live. Breathe free. I rouse myself. Feelings stammer through me, slightly out of synch with my ability to understand them.

'…Yes, I do believe you're catching a cold,' the missus decides, mistaking my shivers.

You snap fully awake. Where – what day is it? Am I still feeling unwell?

'Tomorrow I'll fetch you some antibiotics.' She pats my wrist. Another tender second eases past. 'I know you're not up to getting them yourself, dearie.'

Words like flowers floating on water.

Four days later, when the pain throughout me twists up to an unbearable pitch – my shrill moans upsetting not only the children but the neighbours – I'm finally going to be carted off to hospital. Even through the pain I don't appreciate the thoughtless handling of my bones: to my brothers in law I've already become a bundle of sticks to be chucked into the fireplace. They pay me more respect, though, when I make a puddle of hot tarry vomit just outside the open car door. Then I'm inside Emergency like *that*.

My sense of time narrows to pinpoint stimuli. I subdivide the intervals between the fluorescent lights passing overhead into hours.

*

My belly is reciting an earthquake. Deep tensions released like the bowing of an oboe. The rumbling thunder of my stomach turning foods over and over. Heaving expulsions from one chamber to another. The groaning of imminent farts. Then the gnawing of the bowels begins all over again. Moans resound through the empty cavities of my stomach, hours passing before echoes return…The beautiful machinery of my pain.

The doctor has examined me. He has the results in hand. Yet he sets about probing me again. Superstitious habit, perhaps?

Mounted on his walls are framed oil paintings of white blood cells. The cheerleader laureates are CD4 and CD8. Yay.

I can barely follow his rapid speech. 'Breathe in…?' he asks. I do so. Like sucking in a diseased lung. Oh god. I have pneumonia. I have tuberculosis. I have –

'That hurts,' I say, speaking through a clenched head. The migraine worsens everything. I no longer want to think. Feel. Sense. Anything. The doctor's expression retreats somewhat, like a mistreated invalid. He halts and re shuffles the test results. I can see him revising his thinking until he can hit upon the least bitter way to deliver his verdict. Beating him to the punch, I try joking: 'So, doc, do I have Lung Lint?'

'It's a tumour.'

The known universe wobbles.

'In fact, by living so slow, so still, and in such a metabolically restricted fashion, your immune system has been holding an asymptomatic cancer at bay all these years. It's rare but we've encountered it before: the immune system can corral tiny, dormant growths so that they abide in a kind of vigilant equilibrium.' He laughs awkwardly. 'Any number of us may be strolling around with tumours in equilibrium states! They remain harmless, unless you run out of luck. See, living on the brink of a coma all this time has starved your microtumour of fuel to grow but, uh, the antibiotics for your cold, well, that had a couple of unwelcome side effects. It mucked up the immune system so that it lost intimate surveillance of the tumour, switching off the macrophages that are supposed to be patrolling for new abnormal cells. On top of that, the antibiotics kickstarted your metabolism again, really opened the floodgates.' He shrugs wildly, helplessly. 'This upset the equilibrium your body'd settled on. It's got the jump on us now, I'm afraid. It's spreading fast.' He looks away, touches up his glasses. 'Uh, in fact it's everywhere. It's exploded right through you. Bit of a miracle, what you've done to keep yourself safe so long. Medically speaking, what your body has done for you has only happened once before, so far as we know…'

I stop listening. I think about decay insinuating itself into me, into the interstices between me and more of the rest of me. Cancer, filling up the absence of God with a will the Devil couldn't match. Cancer. Cells with an identity crisis. *Hi. I used to be Peter Bogdanovich.*

The doctor is recommending an expensive though frankly unpromising course of action, something about gamma interferon and regulatory T cells, but I'm still not listening. I already know what I must do.

*

Visiting days are simply too loud – the tramplings of a numberless crowd. Moans travel clear through the hospital walls like anguished whalesong. No privacy to thrash out the wild hereafter of my grief, which, above all, is what I yearn to unload. My soul has become so weighed down. Grief like a pouch of pus warming my heart.

A nurse in a fluorescent white headdress appears. She's here to administer painless small talk to me. Is this the 'talking cure' I've been hearing about? The kindness of her presence gradually dispels my anxiety. Before long I can hear her clearly, though the slow dreamy movement of her lips still disorientates me. The world is slowing down, whereas I'm catching up to it. It's scary. I had no genuine idea how fast daily life had become. I'd caught only bursts.

'I can't understand it!' the nurse cries. 'Your family should have brought you in years ago! How awful, to imagine you were simply sleepy depressed.' *When you were constantly an inch away from death*, the nurse means to add. She's not my usual carer. I suspect these other nurses only visit because they've heard what a medical prodigy I am – unable to live anything approaching a normal life but with a body willing to do anything not to die. They refuse to understand it was my body that fought, not me: I hadn't a clue at any stage. Never had I sensed the cancer, never.

I've always been my body's passenger, a voyeur of my own 'life'.

This nurse is onto something, though: the family is now busy guilt tripping about all their vindictive judgements of me. Hindsight is simply darling, isn't it? Either that or they're defensive about being forced to revise their opinions (opinions tend to set hard, like concrete).

They can only bear to visit me collectively, not singly, face to face. The kids reach me, somewhat: their faces dribble with fear. I endure the new disorder in their enormous sad eyes. It's only to be expected, the poor things. But it's the adults who trouble me more – faces inexperienced at pity now seem disfigured by it. Pah. The patients should have a sign out the front of their ward:

Please Do Not Adjust Your Sympathy:
Normal Cruelty Shall Resume Momentarily.

Only the missus comes alone, last behind the clan.

Our marriage is an insulated tent. We've never let anything touch us. Not even each other, really. If the tent collapses, the empty places of the heart will be sure to join and perish together.

Ah, when she visits she sure brings all the comforts of home…

Of course her remoteness pains me. Agewise, she has a stern sense of being past everything, including mortal illness, she supposes. I can see her deciding to get over me, moving on. The doctor's told her the score: *'Treatment may consume more time than is physiologically plausible…'* And yet, and yet, suddenly unable to say anything because of the intensity of feelings rapidly crumpling her insides to nothingness, she scribbles a quick lipstick kiss across my cheek and flees.

The cacophony of my puny and foolish bladder. The xylophone popping of my knee cartilage as I flex. My bones grinding against their joints like flints striking. The wires of my pubic hairs zinging against each other like a nest of swarming metallic millipedes. The tender fibres of noise whistling in needle thin gales through my blocked nose. The roaring tumours. The expanding universe of my body. The sum of me the sound of my biological functions.

The change in time has been quite, quite, remarkable. Only now can I appreciate sounds outside myself; all sights, sounds, smells in their proper places. For so long have I lived paused in a speed retarded trance, hibernating. I'm having to relearn speech, in a way: after years of long habit I speak too slow. But at last I'm *arriving*, not already here. Truly, I feel free for the first time.

Even if free only to become more of myself. Cancer is more of the same to the *nth* degree. Bad cells growing wild, assuming unlawful size and extension. Rotten through the heart. Rotten through the head. Crazy: *to die of an overdose of self…*My life will rot away tomorrow. Or the next day. It could be that fast. It's galloping ahead, overtaking me, replacing me with my other me. The senseless vacancy of my body. Abdication in favour of rot. Unstoppable rot. 'Life has a compost obituary,' I declared yesterday. 'But self transcendence is current policy!' The missus couldn't grasp me; perhaps refused to. Ah well. I knew what I had to do, anyway. Return to the state of emergency of my past everyday life. *My* normal *everyday life.* Playing for time for the rest of time.

It is four AM on my eighth night in hospital, that hour when the circular calculations of despair claim men, make them suicidal, when I admit to myself I just do not have the heart to die then and there. Not by a long shot. From this point on I refuse all medication. I will check myself out at the next opportunity. Or maybe sooner.

Gathering desperate courage is a universal law. We must all do it one day or another. Make that leap without any grounds for hope. No time like the present. I swing out of bed. It is as if the floor sprays fluorescent cold white-ness against my feet. I'm staggered to find my soul empty, vast; and equally amazed to feel an almost irrational tenderness for myself, at long last. Well, the years soften in their courses. I'm glad for this shot at compassion – it's a freak gift but surrender is welcome. And truly…? Self surrender is the only risk that excites me at this stage.

I make my escape. When I eventually make it home the missus raises an arm in apologetic welcome, not in the least surprised to see me.

Back in my recliner, I stretch out my attention, my consciousness, from days back out to weeks. Like riding a bicycle, can't forget the trick. Seasons dif-fuse back into my bloodstream and slowly expand…

Throughout this slowdown I feel my organs percolating with tiny creep-ing motions, like an internal convection of worms, but it's just the mad-house traffic of my wild cells fighting against the slowdown, resisting still-ness. I'm still turning into my own wilderness, true, but I'm managing to slow down the inevitable. It'll be close, but I think I'll make it…

Whoever wins, me or…'me', by the end I'll be an outlaw within myself. Too bizarre, cancer is. Why does no one ever mention how bizarre it is?

It's drizzling outside. I see a lone fly has come inside to escape the ele-ments. You and me both, buddy.

I have the missus make Maureen take the children elsewhere. No way they're going to witness their old man's fate first hand. The missus loves me for this, leaps to acclaim me as she hasn't for years. Sometimes I catch her wiping tears off her breast. 'Plant your desperate joys in living sorrow,' someone once said. Russian, no doubt.

The missus gives me privacy in this final endless hour. I just recline in this chair and let nature take its course. Once again I'm petitioning silence. Impending isolation spreads like a backdrop of all encompassing low grade fear. The entropic quietening of emotion. But I have a strategy. Cataleptic insomnia or serene resignation, call it what you will. It's my conviction the chronological imperatives of consciousness within this world have *nothing* to do with the mechanics of time and space. If you don't need them – abolish 'em! Bring on the deep gulf that swallows all oblivion. Bring on the night. The void to a million decimal places.

So yes, I abdicate with a will.

There's one place my corrupting body can't touch me. Which is why I'm emigrating.

I'm returning to my thousand year hiatus, that state of near death that buys me time to finish the crossover. I hereby forsake my body to become one with the sound of my biological functions.

With the return to hiatus I'm returning to my real home these sixteen years past: the space between passing moments, the serenity between heartbeats. I'm striving for the state where I'll never reach another heartbeat yet remain free, still me. Springing from nothing, the void will envelop me forever, sustain me in the safety and liberty of timelessness an inch away from eternity. The incommunicable freedom outside time. It is here that I'll take refuge from the cancer of my once begotten body.

The slowdown is going well. The fly has given up flapping its wings and hangs in midair, watching my next move.

The leaves awaiting the fall of sunlight hold themselves still as granite.

The raindrops fall more leisurely, taking their time. Soon I will pause them, too.

It is as if I stand before the event horizon of life, leaning against the very membrane of death itself…at any moment it may give way so that I burst through to the other side. So what is the surface tension of life? What thread is strong enough to moor me here indefinitely, safe from harm while my body rots out from under me?

As I meditate upon the answer a lovely fresh sensation buds crisp upon my cheek. Ah: her kiss has left me but a moment ago.

For Dr Karl

Warrick Wynne

Map of Cannons Creek

This is where we stopped for lunch
at Cannon's Creek that day on the way home.
This is the wooden pier jutting out into the emptiness
at low tide, the creek a thin dotted line
in the estuary, a boat tilted
on its side in the shallows,
mangroves edging out of the sand.

This doesn't show the mosquitoes,
the cheese sandwiches
or what we didn't talk about:
the smashed and crumpled car
back in the towing yard in Moe
that was bright and new so soon ago
and the convergence of these metal things.

Christopher Konrad

Apology of a Lyricist

I

I am sorry for my lyricist my ways sorry am I
My recalcitrant un-anarchic acrylic and gloss-grill lexicon
Deft sweep of glib and refulgent apologetic
Summer sway day play in the heat of my moment and foam
At the very thought of poetic wax and wane

But – what to do in these times desolate of personal mimesis
Water desultory sway in these days creaked crackled and treacle
The sweet of my time my rhyme and play de le langue
It is the French of fence posts and wretched carcases that is my hope
I am sorry for my lyricist my ways sorry am I

II

I start to think, or say I think
Of the sun and its Icarus ways – the nothing to lose
Of endless waves and waves of it over incremental sleep of day

But these semantics refuse the powder red dune after
Ocean of dune: the blessing of Spinifex spike or parched roo carcase
Displayed in naive grey-brown along a never ending desert road

Sun splintered and craggy fence posts stalk my unfinished summer
                                                    memories
As does the cool linoleum of roadside grocery store
Or flies   choc milk under the box tree   lines of buses, four wheelers
And other assorted traveller's trappings

We speak of those times like a vague reminiscence of a future time
As if the thirst of dry roadside sweeps like a river
To a crackled haunt of bare invented imagery fluked like fossils

Frayed like rusted barbed wire and farmers hopes drowned
In the last drought or forgotten politician promises made on the bet
Of someone's next day or   removal from life's smorgasbord

I left thinking   I left speech and my daydreams with you
Entered into a contract with sun and its haunted loneliness
Its coy reluctance to offer me any consolation or joy in my revisionist ways

Rosalee Kiely

'The Heart is a Lonely Hunter'

waiting hunter in a glance dislocates himself: hair weft to flesh
flesh the sleeve caught on a nail
the nail the shock in a mirror of one's own face

started upright by the paddock gate
with a gun on the shoulder in an effigy of man
wrenched and fixated on the silk of his mind
the abject disfigurement of man.

recoils from his strangeness
the vein pocket of night turned inside out

still, fingers of dawn change the sky.
the plinths of feet crackle with frost
a seed melts roots in his chest

then, two boots walk the world home
unlace together and unbutton the clothes
skin, hair, bones lie down. bent to the other one
the faces a mirror. the breath warming chinks to the pillow.

The Heart is a Lonely Hunter is a book by Carson McCullers.

Kailash Srinivasan

Deo Volente

So the man and woman, with their two perfect sons who were of marriageable age, booked a new flat in their younger son's name because the elder one was already burning his blood repaying the loan he acquired for his education two years ago. And so, at least on paper, the younger one at the age of twenty-five owned a property, or two if you considered the couple's first home, whose mortgage had just ended and which would eventually come to the brothers as inheritance in due time. They should have said no to the sales rep who had called on behalf of the builder, with his persistent spiel in a nasal, high-pitched voice, like a drilling machine used on their ears. A polite no would've sufficed, no thanks, we're afraid we won't be able to afford a three bedroom flat, at least not for a few years, and then the short click as the receiver was replaced. But one of their feet was already in the honeyed, oily hands of the masseur. It was only fair to let him do the other foot, too. So they put the phone down, got into the car and went to see the property, fifteen kilometres from where they lived.

'Let's just go and take a look,' said the woman.

The man said, 'We don't need to do anything about it right away. We're just going to take a look.'

There, the rep with a glint of desperation and glee in his eyes, quickly took them to his desk, called for glasses of cold water and hot tea and sat them down on high-back chairs with dirty-maroon cushions. The couple, anxious, looked here and there, smelling the fresh distemper in a hurriedly done up room, dank, which had a name-plate outside that read, Sales Office. The rep, in trousers too tight for him, leisurely pushed the brochure towards them with his delicate fingers and inquired in a keyed-up voice if they knew how fortunate they were to land up at his office today. Only for today, he said, only for them – he said in English that sounded like it had been picked up from *Speak English in 30 Days* – he had a special price. In hushed tones, they switched to their mother-tongue Tamil and went back and forth over the deal. 'Of course,' the man said, 'he will tell us anything to try and trick us into buying.'

'But we also need to think long-term,' said the woman. 'Our sons will soon be getting married, no.'

After a while the rep spoke. But he spoke in Tamil, broken, but well enough to be a shallow character in a cheap novel.

'You have two sons. Two sons! You have *nothing* to worry about,' he said.

'Oh,' they both exclaimed. 'You speak Tamil?' The father drove back home, got his cheque book and handed the booking amount.

To their home, the same evening of their return from the builder's, banks sent house-loan agents to evaluate them and analyse the loan sum they were eligible for. 'Our youngest is the main applicant,' the man told one of them, 'and this one here is the co-applicant.'

'So,' the woman said, 'thirty-five lacs. Possible? Because we want that much minimum.'

'Possible, madam. Very much possible. I'll try for forty.'

He phoned the brothers everyday demanding this and that document, ending the conversations with grand assurances: 'Hundred percent will happen, Sir.' Then weeks passed with no word from him. When the siblings rang him, he would text back saying he was in a meeting and will buzz them in five minutes but never did; or that he was still waiting to hear from his branch manager and hence needed more time. The builder's rep pressed hard with all the pressing his womanly tenor afforded him, seeking concrete dates by when the remaining payment ought to be made and reiterating the repercussions of cancelling the booking. 'Twenty-five thousand will be deducted from the sum of one lac that you've paid.' When the agent finally called, he was subdued, mortified, even. 'Sorry Sir, education loan. Big problem. Only one brother's salary counted, Sir. Only twenty-four lacs.'

'But you promised that...'

'Yes, Sir. Good case yours, but manager said no. But don't worry, Sir. I know this friend who works at *Oswal Housing Loans*. He will charge a commission but he will do it, Sir. Hundred percent he'll do it.'

Despite talking to several representatives and handing over dozens of documents, they got nowhere with the loan sanction letter that the builder needed to proceed with the formalities, until the man, with a Mother Teresa-like disposition and stoop knocked at their door. He scrutinized their documents and cried, '*Arey*, such ignorance.' He held the sides of his puffed face, raised his shoulders and dropped them. 'These yesterday-born, milk-drinking teenagers with curled, wiry-haired beards that banks hire these days. Makes me want to pull my teeth out,' he said. 'Blooding the youth they say. Phasing out the old dogs, they say. For what? So that these *oh-my-look-at-me-skinny-jeans* dolts can douse everyone with their idiocy? Till the day I piss in my pants no one dare touch my desk.'

'So we have a chance are you saying?' the man said.

'Of course, you bloody well do,' the agent said, spraying the man with displeasure-laced spit. 'You listen to me. This is what you need to do. You need to tell the bank that they should also consider your pension. The eligibility will automatically go up.' The man and woman were thunderstruck. The answer was sitting right there on the tips of their noses and they forgot to squint.

Back in three days, the agent with the stoop was frowning unhappily at the cup of tea he was sipping from. Swallowing the last of his tea he placed the ceramic cup and saucer on the table. He shoved his right hand into his pant pocket to keep it from trembling. He inquired about the brothers and was told they were both at work. He seemed to approve of that.

'So, the loan?' the woman said.

He looked at her with mournful eyes and said, 'I resigned from my job this morning. They have already hired some MBA bloke at three times my pay.'

'I'm sorry to hear that but we're actually in a hurry. The builder called again today,' the man said.

'Yes, yes. He will keep calling till he gets all his money. Bloody leeches,' the agent said. 'You know why I quit my job? They would have tossed me out in a few days anyway, but you know why?'

The man and the woman said, 'Tell us. We wonder why.'

'*Broken reed*, if you will, is this man in front of you. How could I overlook it?'

'Overlook, what?'

'The CIBIL ratings. You have a pending credit card payment, Sir, to the tune of sixty-thousand rupees.'

The man, shocked, declared, 'No, I do not,' then said, 'Do I?'

'Also you have defaulted twice on your EMI payments for your present property.'

'Oh.'

'It's all there. So are my failures, out of the crypt. You will not get more than twenty-four or twenty-five maximum.'

'But the mortgage is completely paid out. How does it even matter now?' the woman said.

'Matters to the bank. Shows unreliability. Look at me.'

'So there's nothing we can do?' the man said. 'Twenty-four is no good. With the twenty percent that we have to pay, it still only comes to about thirty-three lacs.'

'Nothing. No longer the lovely, erudite man people came to for advice. Soon I will be fed through an IV tube and dark nurses from Kerala with coconut oil in their black-black hair will give me sponge baths after cleaning my bum. And when people come closer to me they will have a scented handkerchief under their noses.'

'Would you like some more tea?' the woman asked.

'Some scotch, maybe?' the agent said.

'At twelve-thirty in the afternoon?' the man said.

'Why is that so incredible?' the agent said. 'It's funny though, people never drink a one-year old scotch. It's always a twelve- or eighteen-year-old. They call that "beautifully aged". It costs more, too.' He laughed till he broke into a bout of coughing, and said his chest hurt when he laughs too much. 'Tea will do just fine, thank you,' he said.

'Any chance of us getting the booking amount back in whole?' the man said.

'Can I see the papers he drew up for you?' He scanned them quickly and let his eyes rest on the refund clause. 'See, it says so here. Twenty-five thousand processing fee is non-refundable.' He said his only tiny worry was that even if some bank manager was foolishly gallant enough to lend them the money they need and they happen to pay the builder, what guarantee do they have that he won't dust his posterior and take off with the greens? He was, after all, just a project and still did not have much credibility in the market. Brothers deceived brothers and sons murdered their fathers, so what if he was just a phony shamming the working middle-class? He said he even wondered if they would get the booking amount back at all, any of it.

'I'm going to leave you with that thought,' he said, 'and ask you, for what might seem a bizarre requisition. Can I lie down in your bed for a little while? I think if I attempt to take the bus home this moment, I'll just crumble and turn to dust.'

The man dutifully showed him the bedroom where he and the wife slept, which was stacked with a pile of soft-quilts and neck-supporting, doctor-recommended pillows. The agent said he needed to use the bathroom before anything. When he came out, he had slipped into the man's pyjamas that were hanging by the hook inside and left his own clothes there. He asked for a bottle of water that he preferred at room-temperature. He carefully placed his bag and glasses on the computer desk and got into the bed. He told the couple he would appreciate it if they kept their volumes low for he was a light sleeper. 'I will wake up when I have lamented, to my heart's content, over the shrivelment of my usefulness.' As soon as he closed his eyes, he drifted into a dream. In this one, the CEO was at his feet, begging him not to leave. His business will take a hit, he cried. He might even have to shut shop. Later, in the same dream, he was devoting his leisure time to playing a game of bridge at the Poona Club, expensive scotch in hand, surrounded by young agents asking him this and that, looking at him in awe and wonder. 'Super Agent' they called him. There was no case that he couldn't disentangle, not a single Sudoku puzzle he couldn't decipher.

The humour of the situation had waned for the couple. Tensed and uneasy, they sat mutely, tormented by this agent's presence in their personal bedroom. When the agent emerged from the bedroom, nearly two hours later, his mood was pleasant. He went straight to the bathroom and returned after changing into his own clothes. He sat down and said a jolly hello. He plunked his bag on the table, drew out a fresh loan application and a *Reynolds* ball-point pen. 'I will have my scotch now, if you don't mind,' he declared. 'Two cubes of ice, please.'

'Ah, Chivas. You have good taste, Sir.' With the glass of scotch in his hand, he held his chest and laughed. 'Ha-ha, how did I not see this before?' He gave the man a tutorial in investigative journalism, police work, computer hacking, winning a game of cricket. 'There's always a weakness in the opposition's armour,' he snickered. 'The excellent and comforting thing about this is, Sir, is that as long as you're able to dodge the stinkers and patiently wait out for that one sloppy delivery, you have every chance for a win,' he said with a quiver in the flabby, mottled skin under his chin. He seemed pointedly deaf to the subtle signs of restlessness the couple displayed. The man felt compelled to slap the agent and get him out of there. They would have to start the process all over again. Approach some other bank, the rigmarole, the rat running inside of a wheel.

The agent kept tapping the glass with the pen and humming some old-time song that the couple didn't know of, whose tolerance was by now hair-thin. They felt they were being punished for obtusely trusting anyone who remotely resembled hope. *Such a deliberate sadist*, the man thought.

'Frankly, I'm *embarrassed* by this slip-up. You know, it's like going into a war with a blunt sword and expecting to sever heads.'

'Okay, that's all fine. But we need to go for a wedding and if we don't move now we will be awfully late and the couple are one of our best friends,' the woman said. The man looked at his wife in a completely different light, the spontaneity of her mind pleased him, this ingenuity of a fool-proof idea.

'So rude of me to have outstayed my welcome. Just one precious moment of yours and then I'll be out of your hair. It's my years of carefully carved reputation at stake.'

At least the man was moved somewhat. He replaced his imaginary hammer into the tool box.

'Thank you. Can you guess the loophole I just chanced upon?' The couple couldn't.

'Have a look at my trump card then. You will tell the bank…that you will be using your pension money to pay the remaining sum of your elder son's education loan. And this way…'

'The bank will have to consider the entire salary of both my sons, thereby increasing the loan amount,' the man said. 'That's possible, right?'

'*Deo volente*,' the agent said, on his feet and picking up his bag.

The solution was so unexpected, the couple shivered with fear and held on to each other.

'Keep the form ready. I'll pick it up on my way to work tomorrow.'

The couple strained their eyebrows.

'I'm withdrawing my resignation. That MBA kid would have to work harder than that to claim my place.'

So the couple sat down and began filling the form once more, and then realised, the agent's *Reynolds* pen was with them.

Chris Palazzolo

Appointment with an Orphic Headhunter

The left indicator is flicking. How can that be? I indicated right. I clearly remember it. This intersection is so dangerous, people drive like idiots through it. I hate them for it. Inconsiderate rubbish. I always take extra care. I never drive like them, especially if I'm turning right. Maybe it was the impact? My hand dropped involuntarily on the indicator stem and pushed it down? Or the warning lights were just forced on by all the metal crumpling in, which means both indicators are flicking? I can't tell. All I can see is the back corner of the car and it's the left indicator flicking. There it is. The evidence. I was the one in the wrong. It's not fair. I was so careful. I didn't see the other car coming. They run the stop sign. Strange how I know what's happened. But I really didn't see anything. I don't even know what the other car looks like. I don't even know if it was a car. It could've been a truck. I didn't see a thing. Just a quick flit of shadow in the corner of my eye, and then…

I'm here, sitting on the kerb of the traffic island in the middle of the road, looking at the back corner of my car, my lovely new car. Just had its first service last week. $500. Now it's ruined. At least I think it's ruined. I can't see any more than the corner. I can't look at the rest. I can't move my head. My neck is all stiff from the impact no doubt. I can see the back wheel. It's up on the kerb. The indent in the bottom of the tire. Always fascinated me, since I was a child. Weight of the car, calculated by grams of air pressure times square millimetres of indent space. What a strange thing to think about. Petrol is dripping underneath the bumper. Streaming down the concrete kerb. It could blow up any moment. I can't smell it. I can't smell anything. Shock. I can't hear anything either. Tinnitus squeals like two dentist drills on my eardrums. I suppose traffic is starting to bank up behind me. I can't tell. I wish I could stand up and go and turn that indicator off. It's untidy. I hate untidiness. It's lazy, leaving your indicator on. I'll just get up to switch it off. Can't! Can't move! Alright, just sit here, stare at that red pulse, watch the petrol dripping. I can time it. How long before all the petrol drains out. How long before the battery goes flat from the flicking indicator. It's infuriating. Flick, flick, flick, flick, flick, flick, flick…

Look at that train speeding across the level crossing. More inconvenience for drivers. Waste of tax-payer's money those trains. Most people want to drive. Let them do what they want. Too much government running our lives. Hello, here we are, at last. A pair of grey-trousered legs. I assume they're attached to a policeman or emergency worker. Can't be certain of anything these days. Excuse me. Another pair. Excuse me. Well, fancy that. Just run straight past. What's that policewoman doing running backwards into the middle of the road. Oh I see. It's the on-coming lane, one arm pointing twelve the other pointing nine. Have to keep the traffic flowing I suppose. What are those flashes? Cameras. Hope they don't expect me to smile. I wonder if I'm hurt? I just can't tell. I don't feel any pain. I'll just have to sit here and wait to be treated. The other driver must be hurt too. Though why he should be attended to first is anyone's guess, it was his fault. Maybe they have to cut him out of his car? Maybe they can see I'm okay for now, sitting here, in shock, but otherwise unharmed. Another two pairs of running legs, red stripes down the trousers, ambulance. I wish I could call out, make a sound. Hello. I'm just here. Anyone notice me. I'm the driver of the other car. I'm the innocent one, you know the one doing the right thing. God. Just run straight past. It's true, it's the criminals and the undeserving get the special treatment. Us law-abiding folk have to sit and wait. Oh well, I guess I should just be grateful. I'm alive. I don't think I have scratch on me. Just a bit of shock.

Look at that. Another train. Waste of money. Ramona's always on my back about catching the train to work. I'll never catch a train. All those Aboriginals. I'm not racist, but really. Is it absolutely necessary that I be subjected to all that foul language. And they're dangerous too. Everyday there's another report of a bashing. Hello! Good god, it's like they can't see me. Policewoman's getting that traffic going. Life going on around me. Why can't my life go on as well?

Good god. Something's hit my car. Good god. Looks like its front is being seized by a tyrannosaurus.

Oh that's better. I can move my head now. Oh. The world's all slipping around. Come on, get it together. Focus on things. Two police cars. Blue lights flashing. An ambulance parked just behind me. Pretty bad accident. Policeman running yellow tape along the road. Windscreen cubes speckle the road, a twisted piece of bumper lies on the verge. Wonder if that's mine or his? A small group of people standing on the footpath watching. None of them is looking at me. One of them's holding a child!

Hullo, I can stand up too. Just like that, I'm standing, so easy, blinking in the morning sun.

What are they doing to my car. A big red dinosaur jaw jabbing and biting at the cars. The bonnets and doors are literally quivering. They look like living flesh. I still can't hear anything. The movement is violent enough. Better get out the way. I think I'll cross to the verge. Those people are moving off, covering their ears with their hands. Guilty gouls had your fill. Might as well have a look, see what they've seen. My god. He's gone. Poor sod. Christ! Still pulling bits of car…Blood…Don't look! No one's paying any attention to me. I think I'll go home. I think I'll surprise Ramona. It isn't that far. Down on the other side of the highway. Lovely day for walking. I need the exercise. I suppose I should get my case. Can't be bothered. Got a copy of the report on my PC. Wonder if they'll stop me when I go past this cordon? That'll be a good test. Better go under it, don't touch it. Nup. No one noticed. I feel like turning and shouting 'My taxes pay for these services!' I won't though. To tell you the truth I'm glad they haven't noticed. There's nothing wrong with me. If they want me to make a statement they've got all my details in the car. Call me later. Right now I feel like a long walk.

What a lovely footpath. Lovely day, the sun is shining, fluffy white clouds. Houses and gardens look fresh and green. Birds are probably twittering, bees buzzing. I can't hear these things of course. But still, despite that, I feel great. Clear, light. I feel like twenty years has just dropped off me. Worries? What worries. I know this is shock. But I might as well enjoy it. What a mess though. Both cars complete write offs. I couldn't even tell where my car stopped and his car started. Even looked like they pulled the poor bastard's body out of my car. When I get to that street corner I'll look back and make sure. Ooh look, an old Italian lady popped out to see what's going on. She's seen me at least, she's watching me approach.

'Good morning,' I say in my cheeriest voice, and beam my sunniest smile.

Well, how rude can you be! The old witch did the sign of the cross and scuttled back up her driveway.

'Excuse me!' I shout after her. 'Save that for the dead thank you!'

That was a bit of an off-note. I don't feel so great now. I'm really upset about this. No one's offered me any help. I'm going to write to my local member when I get home. The sun is still shining on this footpath though. I can still enjoy the day. And Ramona will look after me when I get home. Dear Ramona. I'll lie down with her when I get back. Cuddle her. Just to sleep. Because I'm very tired all of a sudden. The road looks so long. The footpath stretches to that vanishing point of trees and powerlines. That's not even half way to the highway. And then there's about two kilometres along the highway. Oh well, one foot then the other, that's the way one gets from a to b.

Another train. Go on, mock me. Go on. Ramona's right. If I'd caught the train I'd be at work now. Listening to Ryan and Teresa flirting and surfing the net when they should be doing those KPIs. Kids. Efficient but without a clue. I miss them now. I really want to see them again. I want to say positive things to them, that they'll remember. Things like, 'you'll do well in life as long as you work hard and keep out of trouble.' Advice of an elder.

Here's the street corner. Just up to that power pole. There. Now I'll take another look. Can't see much from here. The ambulance is obscuring the cars. Blue and red lights still flashing. There's the tow-truck bumping up on the kerb, doing a u-turn. I suppose they have to clear it up pretty quickly. I might get into trouble. Leaving the scene of an accident. I'm only about 50 metres down the footpath, they haven't stopped me yet. I was in shock, I'll say. I didn't know what I was doing. Actually, someone has noticed me. That man, standing in front of the tow-truck. He's staring at me down the footpath. He's going to come after me no doubt, gently guide me back to the ambulance. Nice to be noticed. Yep, here he comes walking towards me. He's definitely looking at me. Wonder who he is? He doesn't look like police or ambulance. Just some Joe. He's striding towards me very briskly. I'm not sure I like the look of him. What's he wearing? Steel grey trousers, a sports jacket. He's got no shirt under the jacket. He's bare-chested, barefoot too. He's a bloody hobo. Look at that black messy hair. He needs a haircut. I don't think I want to meet this man. I'll just keep walking, maybe he's not after me. He's still coming, to me, he's coming. I think I'll run. I don't want to see him. He's getting closer and closer. Oh my god. He's going to catch me. He's…he's slapping me, ow, I can't believe slap me in the face he stinks poarr he's panting as he hits me never before never before such indignity in broad daylight I scream ah no help help please stop. I'm crawling at his feet away from him the footpath under my nose Ramona Ramona how will I get home. I'm weeping, yelping, can't help it. He boots my backside, I sprawl face first on the footpath. The indignity. The shame. Cars drive past. No one stops. I'm facing his ugly pinched whiskery face, squinting eyes, fists bunching up my lapels.

'Where do you think you're going?' A nasty nasally sneering voice jars my ears. I can smell too. His breath stinks like a dead cat.

'Home!' I blubber. 'I'm going home!'

'No you're not!' He laughs in my face, poarr the stink. He turns me roughly to face forward.

'You see just over there. You see that guy standing there on the next street corner? That's as far as you'll get. To him. You'll be back at the intersection, you'll walk back up to him. Then you'll be back again. And that's what you'll do till you're gone.'

I stare at where he's pointing. There is a man standing there. I hadn't noticed him before. It's all open space around that corner, so surely I would've seen him walk up. Either way, it's another man I don't want to meet. He's dressed in jeans and tee-shirt and he's also barefoot. He seems to have some kind of shadow over his head, even though he's in open sunshine. Maybe it's a flaw in my eye. His head looks all spread out, like a ball of plasticine smeared by a giant thumb. My heart is pounding from these shocking events. But that fellow is the scariest thing I have ever seen.

'You've met him before. He's the other driver. Bad luck for him, he popped off too early. You're in luck though. You haven't quite gone yet. You have to hurry. You have to catch 'em when they're coming. Follow me.'

I don't know what he's talking about, but I follow him. He seems a safer bet than that creepy fellow down the road. I follow him across grass and weeds of the corner up to the wall of a nearby villa. He climbs up and over the wall. I can't do that. Trespassing.

'Come on, hurry!' he calls from the other side. 'You've only got a few seconds!'

I climb over the wall. It is so easy, I feel so light. I land nimbly in the narrow courtyard. I follow him around the corner to a bedroom window. He peers in the window, through the security grill, his hands cupping his face.

'Who are you?' I ask him.

'I work for the Orpheus Consortium,' he says without looking at me. 'You're my commission.'

He turns to face me, presses his shoulder and hip against the window, and vanishes. The window does a little shudder. I blink. What? He kind of slipped in, erased, like a screen with a string behind that you drag across. I go up to the window and look through the grill and flyscreen. I can see the edge of the sliding window. It is open ten centimetres. His furious face appears at the window.

'Come on, idiot!' the white teeth snarl behind the grill. 'Come on! Just press your shoulder here, HERE!'

I do as he says. I feel the mesh of the grill on my shoulder. This is ridiculous. I'm solid, I can't…

                       With a disgusting sensation of a farting plop, I'm inside in stuffy gloom. A double bed, good god! Two people having sex. This is disgraceful. How did I get here. I'm terribly sorry, I don't know what came over me I was just walking home this man forced me to enter your house please forgive me I'll just leave…shove in the back towards the bed.

'Go on, quickly! Under the sheets!'

It's dirty, disgusting, perverted, I can't. I lift up the bottom sheet. I slide in under between their legs four bare foot heels butting my head shoulders chest hips knees

                   not pushing myself

                             lashed to a gleaming pole size of a lamppost hammering up suffocating pulpy seal can't breathe

                   can't breathe vagina stink

               seized whole body arms legs flailing

      dumped wave sea

                     semen rush…

*

The siren screams through the ambulance cabin. The medic freezes, mid-compression. He stares at his blood-caked hands, pressed palm on knuckles on the smashed chest. The scrape of snapped bone seems like an unnecessary indignity now. The old boy is dead.

Yannis Hondros

Abrolhos Man

He might have followed
the devil himself
into this nameless place

only to be abandoned
along the coastal penumbra
up to the Kaanya tree

dressed as emperor
the giver of souls
to be undone from high

bound and strung up
hardened in the sun
along with yesterday's fish

the frail white bone
buried not deep enough
to hide a second skin

his arms in a half circle
a sand angel sweeping
four long centuries

hands severed then
placed beside his head
mourning over him

while dusting the past
reveals the long slivers
of sharpened bone

his skull a grey firkin
for fish-bone and crab
twisted, punished and caulked

Peter Jeffery

We Are Half Cousin to the Fish

On the Lido, small black Romans eat the fruits of the sea,
Spiked anemone, mussel eye and whorled sea snail.
Still dripping salt water as held between the fingers,
They are gulped down as a groper,
Blind with huge dull eyes, mumbles weed on rocks,
Till sated, they belch and flop away
In a dribble of towels and flapping thongs.

But in Ostia the small brown Romans
Dived deep into the element,
With the alertness of a gull sighting flake of fish.
Water held as their port in the hands of the sea,
Thus cradled and rocked, they watched
The sad dying of dolphins in nets,
Or the squids cast down on the mosaics.

No wonder they were brothers to the sea,
And saw the huge marriage feast of Neptune
Where nymphs and horses and gods trailed tails,
Sexual, rhythmic and pulsing through water,
Their proudest stance
Was prone or diving down
Into the raptures of the deep,
Where, in bronzed love, these water gods
Laughed ripples of minnows from their mouths.

Toby Davidson

Sunset, Cottesloe

Speckled in sand and stinking sun
we salivate that last longitudinal pluck
of an indigo harp at a lion's skin
dragging the gold of its kill to its keeper:

Africa. Watching us. Pupiless. Ochre-lipped
in the East, bronze-tailed in the West
and vice versa as we bluster about
the old drum-skull of the infinity stream,
milk teeth gnashing corners from our towels.

Salts of the earth, Gage Roads, hems of spheres
touch, taste, singe, unable to conjure
the comfortable distance of travel ads.
Breeze, barely one coat of air, opens
lapis lazily…We feel you in our fingertips,
in our lips' diverging gulls.

Richard James Allen

The Secret Oeuvre of Our Man on the Street

Why did he walk? Who

    knows? He walked. Aimlessly, thoroughly,

      for miles

      around the

    forgotten   parts of the city. He walked past what was

      new

      and

      what was old. And what was in between,

                  like gaping

              holes where

    teeth have been pulled. He took

   photographs with his memory. One

          day

      he'll   develop and print them, and we'll know

what   he saw.

Harold Mally

My Wife, the Novelist

People don't realise what a warzone it is in business these days. After spending the day in the firing line, shooting off emails and doing my best to kill off the competition, I battle the traffic to return to home base. I love military analogies, as do all of our management team. I've never actually been in the military, nor, to my knowledge have any of my colleagues. But we all appreciate how an effective campaign can rally the troops. And really, the analogies are appropriate. Everything really is a battle; we live and die by our decisions. We kill our competitors off, we destroy targets. We are lean, mean, fighting machines. It's all true. The baby food industry is a battlefield.

After fighting the good fight all day I park my car in the garage and march into the house as usual. I am surprised to see my wife Louise sitting on the lounge, a look of stunned disbelief on her face.

'Lou?' I say tentatively. There is no reaction. 'Louise? Is something wrong?'

She looks up, as if it has only just registered that I am standing in front of her. 'No,' she says in a faraway voice. 'Nothing's wrong.' She waves a typewritten letter at me. 'I can't believe it,' she says after a further pause. 'They're going to publish my novel.'

Louise had always considered herself to be a writer, but she was a writer who never wrote anything. When at university she studied English Lit and had had vague notions of one day writing a novel. But instead of writing she married me and had children. While I climbed the corporate ladder Louise juggled her time between working in menial clerical jobs, while raising two children and running the household. I think she was a little disappointed in herself because she never really amounted to anything in her career. I always explained that it didn't matter so much because one high flyer in the family was enough. It was good that she had an income to supplement mine, but let's face it, Louise has never had the killer instinct required to really make it in the big time.

She had never thought that she would fall into the same pattern of behaviour as her mother's generation. She had expected that we would both have satisfying careers, but somehow the reality was that she looked after the kids while I went to work, just like her mother and grandmother and generations of women before that. She should take some solace in the fact that our daughter is a high flying commodities trader. She should realise that our parenting has enabled her to do that. But somehow, over the years, she seemed to have developed a kind of belief that she had lacked achievement in her own life.

So when the kids left home she decided to do what she had always wanted to do, which was to write. She had found it remarkably easy to get back into the rhythm of writing fiction, even though she had not done so since her student days.

She wrote short stories and sent them off to a number literary journals. Before long she was a published author and a little while after that a story of hers won an award. The small emoluments that she received for her efforts, while satisfying from an ego perspective, in no way threatened her amateur status.

After two years of short story writing, Louise decided to do what she had been planning to do from the first day that she started banging away on the keyboard: she started to write a novel. By this time she was also a member of a writers' group. I don't know what the writers group actually did, I just think it was a latter day equivalent of a sewing circle, but one of the other members recommended an agent. The agent, an energetic young woman named Coleen, was enthusiastic about her work. I think Coleen was laying it on a bit thick, but that was her job I suppose. Anyway, she must have done her job pretty well because here is Louise with the letter in her hand. It is true. Her novel is going to be published.

'Wow, that's great. How about that?' I say, although I am a little suspicious. You hear about so many scams these days. 'Um, this isn't one of those deals where you pay for the printing and they spell your name wrong on the cover is it?'

'No. It's a major publisher.' She thrust the letter at me. 'Martin. It's the biggest publisher in the country. They're even paying me an advance.'

'That's great, Lou. I always knew you could do it. Hey. We're gonna have to celebrate. Have you told the kids yet?'

I have always been supportive of Louise's writing. Right from the start, when she told me of her plans in the writing area I always gave her little motivational speeches. I'd tell her that she had what it takes, that she could do it, that she just had to release the writer within her in order to destroy the writing game. It was the same kind of talk that so successfully motivates my staff at work. I shouldn't be surprised that my motivational techniques worked so well, but Louise only appeared to listen half-heartedly and return to her computer. But, you have to pay results. Even though she did not seem to pay attention, my motivation techniques obviously had some effect because she kept at it and now she is going to be published by a major publisher.

It's funny how these things happen. It is good for Louise to have an interest. When she took it up I supported her because it gave her something to do, something that could give her a sense of achievement. Self-respect is very important for people. She could have joined a tennis club or played golf or taken up pottery. It would have been all the same to me. But she chose writing. As worthless as this might have seemed to some, I still supported her as if she was doing something that had intrinsic value. So, for something like this to come of it is totally unexpected.

Whenever any of her stories were published I always read them. Of course I couldn't be bothered reading the other stories in the magazines. They were just little small circulation publications anyway. Not things that most people would read. There was never anything of a military or motivational nature in them. The only people who would read them were probably just other aspiring writers who contributed to the same magazines.

I am by no means old fashioned. I believe in women's rights and all that. When we were married, Louise changed her name to Grantham, my surname. Not because I thought she was my possession or anything like it. It was really just for the sake of the children. And my career. It would have looked weird for a high flying executive in the cut throat world of the baby food industry to have a wife with a different surname. It just would not have suited the family values of the organisation.

But when she started to write she reverted to her original name of Louise Moore. I had no problem with that when she was publishing stories in little magazines that nobody read. Now she is going to have a book published by a major publisher under the name of Louise Moore. I am not sure how I feel about that. I am not sure how it would go down at the office. Would I be judged as somehow weak because my wife was using her pre-married name? I have to think about this.

A few months pass and nothing seems to change. The lag times in this book writing business are horrendous. I'm used to the cut and thrust of the corporate world. Instant feedback is the order of the day. You have to strike while the iron is hot. He who hesitates is lost. But with this writing stuff, it's just all waiting around for something to happen. It was bad enough with these short stories. She'd send something off and if you were lucky three months later it would appear in a magazine. How are you supposed to keep someone motivated with a time lag like that? The whole industry needs a shake-up if you ask me.

So while nothing is happening on the publication front I continue to do battle on the field of commerce every day. Louise, for her part, continues to work part time in her office and spend her out of work hours writing stories. She continues to write short stories and send them to small publications.

I try to give her the benefit of my experience in industry. These are things I know about. I advise her that now that she is going to have her own novel published she could sell her short stories for higher prices. She should stop sending them to these small time publications. I'm afraid that the pending publication of her book does not seem to have increased her self-esteem any. She says that the whole idea is not to make money, but just to get things published so people could read them. I am sure she is just rationalising and try to tell her that she should not sell herself short like that. She has a marketable commodity and she should not be scared about selling it for what she can get. I am a little frustrated by her lack of understanding. In spite of this frustration, I am still proud of her effort and praise her accomplishments to friends and colleagues whenever the opportunity arises.

Then one day, after spending all day defusing a potentially explosive labour relations scenario, I return home to find Louise sitting on the sofa talking to a journalist and photographer from the local newspaper. They have been interviewing and photographing on the eve of publication of her first novel. They can obviously see that I've had a busy day and soon after I arrive they say they are all done and are about to go. I am not at all put out by their presence. There is no need to leave, I tell them. They should continue. In fact I have a number of suggestions that could improve their article. But they are very polite. They don't want to take up any of my time and any more of my wife's. I can see why these two are only working for a local paper. They don't have the killer instinct to make it in the cut and thrust world of big city journalism. They have the opportunity to get a better angle, but they are just too polite to take it up. And when they leave they call me Mr Moore!

The newspaper article is all about a local writer who made good and includes a very positive 'exclusive' review of the soon to be published book. I am pleased with the article. The journalist is more highly skilled than I had realised. She makes Louise sound witty and intelligent. Obviously it would have been better if they had made some mention of the encouragement of her husband, who supported her writing in spite of his highly demanding executive position, but overall it's not too bad.

Following that first foray into the press, Louise's agent Coleen works hard to get the book into the pages of the media. She forwards copies of the article to the literary as well as the mainstream city press. She also arranges for a website to be designed, as well as publicity from the publisher.

After the interminable lag time between the book being written and accepted for publication, suddenly everything is happening at once in a prepublication rush of activity. Louise has no sense of perspective on these things. Coleen is doing a good job in getting her publicity, but Lou still seems shy about it. I do my best to keep her motivated, tell her to embrace the opportunity, grab it with both hands, don't let it slip away. I give her the benefit of all of the profound things that I have read and heard in so many motivation books and DVD's. Louise just says she did not take up writing in order to be a celebrity; she took it up to write.

Once the book is released, there are interviews with print, radio and on-line journalists. There are book launches in different cities and tours of book stores for signings.

Amidst the hive of activity, Louise wakes up one morning to find that her book has reached the best seller lists. She was happy enough just to be a published author. Suddenly she is on the best seller list and there are new demands on her time from journalists seeking her opinion on everything from literature to movies to politics and sport. Now she is being quoted on things she doesn't even have an opinion on. The world has gone crazy.

I won't even go into all of the lost opportunities. After all of this positive publicity Louise now has a real opportunity to cash in. But what does she do? She says she's giving no more interviews, doing no more tours or book signings, instead she's going to sit down and write another book and she doesn't want to be disturbed by the outside world. I have to have a serious word with her.

When you have a passion for something, if you are really going to succeed in that thing, you need to embrace the entire thing, not just one part of it. Like baby food. I have a passion for baby food. Now it's not just the product, it's the baby food experience in its entirety that I am passionate about. The manufacture, the marketing, the design of the jar, the market research, the nutrition, the placement on supermarket shelves. All of these things and a myriad of others make up the baby food experience. Now as someone who is passionate about baby food, I am passionate about every one of these aspects.

It's the same thing with being a writer. Writing is not just about sitting at a keyboard and banging away. That is just one aspect of it. There is a market there as well and you have a commodity that you have to get to market. If you are passionate about writing you have to have that same burning desire for every aspect of the writing experience, from book title to jacket design to getting poll position on the bookstore shelves.

I explain all this to her. It's like talking to a brick wall. She just doesn't get it. I don't try to tell her how to write. I'm no good at that. She's the writer. But the business aspect of the writing game is something I can help her with. I don't know how her agent puts up with her. I am close to despair.

But that's not the worst of it. I've always been into music. I have imparted my love of rock music to our son Pete. While Louise carped on that he was wasting his time, I encouraged him to do an audio engineering course. I took him to gigs when he was young. I bought him his first guitar and taught him his first rudimentary chords. Now that he's a music producer, what does everyone say? He gets his creativity from his mother. From his mother? She had nothing to do with it. She opposed it. I'm the one who's been behind him all the way.

And what makes everyone think that Louise is so creative? I mean, what's she done really? Okay she's written a book. One book. I've been on the creative cutting edge day in and day out for years. Keeping out in the forefront of the baby food industry requires a constant stream of creativity. Who changed the colour of our labels and increased our market share by five percentage points? Five whole per cent, just by a simple change in the colour of the label. But that means nothing. The only thing that matters is that one book.

I'm not sure what she has been doing. A book signing or a radio interview or a public appearance at a writers' festival. Whatever. Anyway, she is surprised when she returns home to find me on the lounge playing my guitar. She looks at me strangely.

'Is something wrong?' I ask.

'What's that?' She points to my new axe.

'A Strat. A Fender Strat; just like Hendrix used to play.'

'I've never known you to play a guitar before.'

'Just because I haven't played for a while doesn't mean I'm not committed to it. I have this need to express myself creatively,' I say in an off-hand kind of way.

'We've been married for thirty years. This is the first time I've seen you with a guitar.'

'Well, you're going to see a lot more of it,' I say. 'I really feel the creativity flowing through me.' I bash out a few chords and Louise walks out of the room with her hands over her ears.

'Pete. I need your help. I want to record a demo.'

'A demo? Don't you have a company that records all your commercials?'

'I'm not talking about a baby food demo. I want to do a music demo. I've taken up guitar again. I need some studio time to put together a demo tape.'

'You don't need a studio. You can do it all on a computer. You record it as MP3 or .wav files. You can burn it to CD if you want, but it's probably easier just to email the files if you need to send them to anyone.'

This is why I contacted my son. He's a professional at this sort of thing. He knows about the latest up to date technology. I knew all that encouragement and mentoring I gave him would pay off.

So I take my new Strat and Marshall amp over to Pete's place. He is surprised to see that I have grown a goatee and my hair is not as short as it used to be. It is not actually long. I can't grow it long. It wouldn't look right in the office. But it is longer. And darker.

'What's with the new image?' he asks, then he sees what I am carrying and forgets about me completely. 'Hey, cool guitar. When did you get it?'

We talk a bit about guitars and guitar players and I tell him my plan. I tell him about how I've got all this music bottled up inside me just bursting to get out. I tell him how I want to record a demo tape, sorry, some demo files and send them out to record companies. Then maybe I'll form a band and go on the road.

'Hey Dad,' says Pete. 'No offence, man, but nobody's going to be interested in listening to a fat sixty year old who's just learning to play guitar.'

I suck in my stomach. 'Hey man. I'm not fat and I'm not sixty.'

'Okay, a fifty-eight year old.'

'And I'm not just learning. I'm relearning. Just getting back into it, that's all. Don't forget who taught you that E minor eleventh chord.'

'Hey dad, you've been getting a bit weird lately. Just because mum's a successful writer now, it doesn't mean that you've got to compete. She's doing her thing; it's cool. Just leave it at that.'

'This has nothing to do with your mother's writing. I don't know what's wrong with everybody. The whole world doesn't revolve around that book you know. You don't realise Pete that we've both had this dream to slow down and do what we really want to do. Okay, your mother got a head start. She was able to slow down earlier, but the baby food industry is a cutthroat world. I couldn't just walk out on my obligations. I had to transfer some of my experience and expertise to other people before I could even think about slowing down. Even now I'm still working long hours, keeping everything afloat. But I can't wait any longer. The need to create is just too strong.'

I really don't know what it is with people. Louise is lucky that she has had me to mentor her into becoming a successful writer, because she certainly has no vision. It seems to be the same with Pete now. We used to share rock dreams, but now he appears to have lost the vision as well.

He grudgingly agrees to record my new songs. At the end of the session I am totally pumped. I know I'm not a great singer, but that doesn't matter. It's the energy and passion that I put into the music that makes it so outstanding. I've laid down ten tracks and Pete is speechless. The emotional experience must have been too heavy for him.

Louise is in London. There's some big awards ceremony she has to attend. Her second novel has been short-listed for one of those literary prizes.

Kind of like the Oscars, only for boring people. I couldn't go to England. I couldn't leave the company in the lurch like that. Sure, my boss told me to go and share Louise's triumph. But I know he was only saying that. The place would fall apart without me. And anyway, what chance has she got of winning?

I've just returned home from a night of busking. I played for hours. I played all my new songs, but nobody was interested. Okay, I thought, they don't know my songs. So I played some covers, things that people would be familiar with: Beatles, Stones, Animals. They crossed the street and walked on the other side. Nobody threw me any money, nobody stopped to listen. Everybody gave me a wide berth. I've reached a new low point in my life. I thought I'd be able to destroy this music scene, but nobody wants to listen.

The phone rings. It's Louise calling from London. She sounds drunk.

'Martin. Have you heard?'

'Heard what?'

'I won. Darling I won.'

'That's great, Lou. You deserve it.'

'Has it been on TV over there, yet?'

'Ah, not yet. I'll just turn it on and have a look.'

Well, that's it. She won. I'll spend the rest of my life playing second fiddle to my wife the novelist now. As if they'd play some book award on TV. I turn it on anyway.

Sure enough, there she is.

'…and I owe it all to my husband Martin. I really couldn't have done any of this without him. He's supported me all the way and he's always given me career advice. He believed in me when nobody else did. If it wasn't for his sacrifices I could never have written this book.' She holds up the pseudo Oscar, looks straight at the camera and says, 'this is for you, Martin.'

Suddenly it all goes crazy. The phone is ringing and there is pounding on the door. The entire country's media seems to be on my doorstep.

'Martin, Martin,' they call out.

'What do you think of your wife's success?'

'What's it like to be the man behind a great writer?'

'What kind of advice did you give Louise?'

I take a moment to gather my thoughts.

'Let me tell you,' I say. 'The literary world is like a warzone. You have to attack it like a military campaign.'

Damon Lockwood

City Rubber Stamps

1.

She became suspicious at his fourth visit inside two and a half weeks. A regular customer was perhaps three times a year.

'Three dollars sixty five thank you…and, um…what are you doing?'

'It's…I…'

From the beginning, their relationship was fated with a startling mediocrity.

2.

Their love making was always stiff and full of corners. Actual consummation took some time because he always started too early. For the entire month of May he spurted stupidly into his hands whenever she took even the least piece of clothing from herself.

He would stand there, his cupped hands full of spunk, an unpleasant look of shame and release scratched across his heaving face.

And even when he gasped 'You're just so…beautiful', it never seemed to ease the moment.

3.

She never let him stay the night, and she had no desire to see his house – that would be all too upsetting to bear. She needed him to leave so she could stand in front of the mirror and again contemplate the confusion of her life.

4.

At home, at night, three to four hours after leaving, she couldn't believe the actual place existed. A pale blue, brick, one room building on the edge of a crumbling car park, near the North-East side of town. Selling rubber stamps.

Three hours after leaving the place it just didn't seem possible.

5.

'You know those stamps you order for me – you know I see them before you pick them up and give them to me, right?'

'I thought they might make sense, you working there and all.'

'Surely you must realise they're the last things I want to see after leaving the place.'

'What about the one that says "be my teddy bear"...and it's shaped like a teddy bear?'

She wondered, behind her lowered glasses, whether it was in fact possible to cry without tears.

6.

She saw her boss once a month. After three years she was convinced he still didn't know her name.

'Well then, keep up the good work...and...with the...'

After three years she was still waiting for a reason to steal something she sold.

7.

She was standing in her limp green kitchen, looking out the window. He shuffled behind, standing aimlessly. Explosions often occur aimlessly.

'We could fire-bomb the place.'

Outside the window a blade of grass twitched in the dampening grey. She turned to find him looking at her.

She wrapped her mouth around his cock, groaning as she pulled deeply.

First time given, first time received.

8.

Perched next to him, researching how to make fire-bombs, she felt the first inkling of what it is to be in love.

Wondering about actual possibilities, he felt the first stirrings of what it was to be himself.

9.

They executed the plan seamlessly. Stamps fell around them like confetti. Rubber stoked the blaze.

Running away in their self-made black outfits, she stumbled and came up bleeding.

Bending down to her, he was amazed to discover this incredible woman laughing her fired-up eyes out.

10.

The morning sun spread across the lake they were sitting next to like honey. Ibis pecked in the foreground.

'You know', he said, resting back on his elbows, 'I always hated my fucking high school.'

She smiled. The sun pricked its way up her warming toes. She wondered if she would wear red to their wedding.

Robbie Coburn

There Are No Strangers

There are no strangers past the lookout post of the farm;
In blankets, the kids size up soft-storm path.

Dogs bark away below the hill
drowned out by puttering drops in miniature springs —

both earth and sky still in the former absentee's wake —
trees shake hands. Rocks run a marathon,

finishing up by the veranda, still
alive and ticking like an electric fence.

Night encases the empty sky, indistinct amidst symphony.
I can scarcely hear myself breathing.

Home suspended on brass hinges,
I ignore all motion. Alive.
My hands have disappeared in front of me-

There is beauty in that.

Lorne Johnson

Visionary

Royal North Shore's
chief eye guy
informed me I had a
blow out in left orbit
after the Riverina Cowboy,
fueled by whiskey gusto,
cracked my eye socket
with fists remade in Redfern.

During rituals of die
and light, in bleached
boxes thick with *what ifs*,
I tried to cultivate wholeness
by dreaming of event horizon
festivities, dust might, singing
matter, white holes — any universe
verse to restore my humour.

Andrew Bifield

After the Bucks' Night

I

More than nine months passed: our great objections
Had deflated. I won money on
The timing of the news. They had gone
Through six months more than nine of our dissections
By the time the child was due. We laughed,
Drank, drew conclusions; had a brief return
To form: three months more, there was a turn,
And the baby wasn't born.

II

The notice said bright colours: most wore Hawaiian
Shirts. The priest was an old broom, wooden and tall;
The church was brown and modern, and small.
So was the coffin. The sky had rolled from cyan
Into grey as the directors gave
Cards out at the door. Someone up back
Disrupted the service with a heart attack.
The disapproval waved
Through the church, because they didn't know;
And at the wake they realised. It was the real show.

Mike Greenacre

Skeleton

I laid it out as a jigsaw
on his dining-room floor,
piece by missing piece
like a cryptic message
creating shape

my father directing
pieces by name and place
as a doctor with his
Anatomy students tidying
loose ends of investigation.

I look at it soaking
in the afternoon
sunlight – bones once
strewn across the growing
rooms from childhood

now a human form: 'The
first time it's been together
in 50 years' he says with
reverence – someone once
loved, now lays here alone.

'The skull is the most
emotional part' – a frame-
work that houses the
ability to see, hear, talk,
and think   admitting

he never looks at the skull
without seeing it
covered in flesh
and wondering what kind
of person lived here.

Aaron Furnell

Crack Den Delight

The table's encircled by fiends
A crack hungry family
'Pack the pipe please, mum,' asks the skinny, ravenous daughter
Slavering in anticipation
As does my cock over her.
The mum packs the pitiful crack.
Dad fills the dank room with burnt sausage smoke
We fill the room with cigarette and crack smoke
As he slaves away upon the stove top
As we feed our drug addictions
Slaving away
No one touches the sausages.
Me and her sit as she plays Assassin's Creed, sexily.
The mum and dad do mum and dad things, at light speed.
'I'm going to watch a movie in my room,' the daughter says.
'Can I come?' I ask.
'Whoever wants can come,' she replied.
She came multiple times, she told me
I couldn't come once
But, fuck, was I sweaty.

Julia Osborne

Maitland's Cow

A mist is settling across the paddocks, following the creek. In the early dawn a fox barks, nearer, farther, going away. The moon is sinking in the west and the last stars have faded.

Steam comes up from the man's spray of piss off the veranda. His feet are cold on the wooden boards. His wife is inside, in the dark warm cave of the room, feeding the baby, holding it against her warm skin, her head bent, almost asleep, curled over the tiny turned cheek. She will come back to bed, long after he's come inside from the veranda, and she'll lie, curved, knees up, feet tucked into the hem of her nightdress, the knuckles of her vertebra going down down and he'll reach over to cradle her and she'll say Uh, uh, irritably, sleepily. He'll mutter, I wasn't going to. That's what it's like these days.

Almost light. Half waking, he leans towards her, wanting, whispering, Sarah. Soon the baby will wake again. His fingers reach, touch; his mouth finds her breast where the soft cotton has dropped aside. His tongue explores, licking, tasting. The duvet rises and is swept away, sheets billow and her feet smack onto the floor. It is an exasperated smack.

Shouldn't have touched her tit. Sacred. For the baby. He hears her washing and knows she's bent over the basin, slipping hot soapy hands around her body, washing away his lick. She doesn't know he can see. The door is open a chink…a glimpse…she leans over the basin and the nightdress swings open. Maitland is unhappy. How can a woman be so tired? Doesn't have to work. What's she on about? She sees into his skull.

'Don't you realize,' she hisses around the half-open door, 'that I'm exhausted? That I'm drained? All my energy goes into this baby, our baby, and you can't hold off for a fuck! You're amazing.'

The door bangs shut. She's kicked it. She mutters angrily. Why is he always watching? My body is my body. Now Lucy's crying.

Maitland lies motionless in the wide bed. His gaze glides vacantly about the room, measuring widths in relation to each other. There is a certain built-in harmony. When you've built the house yourself, your gaze can't let go the proportions of things, the juxtaposition. Draw a line, put that window there. With a few mates in to help, raising the frame's easy. Love that smell of wood. Hours rubbing lanolin into the hands each night, slowly, like a meditation. Sarah used to call it Doing a Lady MacBeth. Will this little hand never be smooth? Where's her humour gone? I thought everything was okay. Come home from hospital, everything's fine. I know she's sore. I keep away. I count six weeks. Give it two months. I keep away.

Now, Sarah sits in the kitchen with Lucy. The door of the wood stove hangs open, the fire warming her, warming them both. Maitland stands at the window, looking across the hills. Sunrise by seven. Cold enough for a heart-starter.

'That's a filthy drink,' she observes from her corner.

He ignores what she has to say about the mug of muscat. She says it often, her nose wrinkling. He got to like it years ago on a camping trip. *Damn cold in the mountains. Mist like potato soup, no way to get warm except get up. Dingos calling, out in the fog. They can't see either. Mate hands me a mug and says Here y'are, get this into you! The tin mug's full. Warms the guts. Warms the heart.*

Early sun touches dew on the grass by the path to the shed, lights up water splashed across the concrete floor. A horse snorts, blowing misty clouds. Dog on his chain by the tank curls tighter, one ear pricked for the sound of the back door opening. Out there milking, leaning his head into the cow's warm flank, Maitland watches his hands streaming the milk into the bucket and thinks of the woman by the kitchen fire. Life's simple for you, Maybellene, he tells the cow, as she stands stolidly, chewing her cud in a clockwise fashion.

While she finishes feeding the baby, Maitland brings in the milk from the brown cow, strains it into jugs and scalds the bucket. The woman watches this clanking of steel. Her husband's back is to her, showing holes in the elbow of each sleeve, with crinkled yarn where it's pulled. His legs look bowed or maybe it's just the skinny legs of his jeans. She has made tea and the rolled oats porridge soaked overnight in milk and left at the back of the fuel stove, is perfectly cooked. When Sarah returns to the kitchen from changing a nappy, he has already gone.

Peace, she thinks. He needs me too much. I haven't that much to give. Not now. Later. Through the window, she sees him striding away, Dog bouncing beside him.

Maitland is going to check the cattle. Today the calves must be separated from their mothers. He has studied all this in his livestock management book, before they left the city. Before buying the block. Excited to be tree-changers.

Maitland catches the horse easily, spreads the checked wool blanket on the curving back and fastens girth and circingle. The straps and buckles are familiar now. Cattle look good, Maitland muses, pausing at the fence, gazing, counting. Better move them out of that paddock, now. Something about paspalum this time of year. Leaning on the pommel, he appraises them. He sees himself in cocked felt Akubra, handsome, likeable. Lonely. Maitland has his hand in his pocket, around the neck of a flask. Just a suck. Helps the time go by. Do the right thing then, and toss it down the sink. You know how it upsets her. Ah, Sarah.

A thin little childish song comes from his lips. *Lavender's blue, diddle diddle, rosemary's green, when I am king, diddle diddle, you shall be queen…*

He musters the cattle, pushes them into the yard behind the shed. They're a fine mob. From there, it's easy to draft calves from cows. Poor Maybellene, you too. I'm sorry. Swing the gate. Cows one side. Calves the other. Mooing. Calling. Push 'em up, Dog!

The calves huddle together, big calves now and time to be sold. The cows will call for several days, then forget. The bull will help them forget. Maybellene has to stay around the house, as milker.

He spends the morning quietly pushing the cows across to a paddock some distance from where he leaves their calves. Between them and fenced off with four-strand barb is limestone country, full of rocks, trees and wild grass covering secret hollows. Where the trunk and branches of an old tree angle and arch, there is a wide, deep hole. Lizards and spiders live there among little pockets of ferns anchored to the walls before the rock drops smoothly to the bottom, with scattered tree debris and bones of small fallen animals.

Maitland rides towards home, sees the white squares hanging in two scooping lines behind the house. While he watches, they are gathered and he enters the house to find Sarah folding all the washing, nappies last. He kisses her cheek and runs water into the kettle. Where he sets it on the stove the drops spit and pop on the hot iron. He opens the fire door to push in another log, but she says, 'No, I want the fire slow, I'm cooking a roast.' He squats there, feeling the fire's warmth on his face. The skin on his mouth is chapped with a little crack forming and dried blood.

Poor lips, Sarah thinks. Hair like silk. The stuff on fresh corn, under the husk. He looks tired. But she doesn't touch him.

'How's Lucy?'

'She's good.'

'Asleep?'

'Asleep.'

'Tea?'

'Thanks.' He pours her a cup of weak black tea and a strong one for himself. Slugs it with a dash from the flask. Hmm. It's been a big day and his body feels weary folded into an easy chair. He crosses his feet, stretches.

'Yuk,' Sarah says. 'Look what you've brought into the house.'

All along his trouser legs are small black specks of ergot from the paspalum. The field will darken day by day with a gradual attrition of colour:

light to dark. Green to grey. Should check the book, see what it's about. The cattle have called during the night, waking him once. I'll get up early, he thinks, check 'em out. And he slides deeper into sleep.

In the night, a fence falls.

In the night, the woman rises from her warm, her snug bed. Her toes pushed into slippers, she stokes the kitchen fire, sits curled over the baby's turned cheek. Snoozes peacefully. How the baby grows, how she is blooming. So beautiful, this little thing, my own one. Mine. Back in her bed, she sleeps, her knuckled back like a shield.

Maitland kicks his way out the gauze door and treads cold-footed into the early day, milk bucket swinging, knocking against his knee. Why is she like this? It isn't me. It's her. Selfish bitch.

Maybellene is not waiting where he locked her last night in the small house-paddock by the shed. Dammit, Maitland curses. I suppose she's wandered off to find her fucking calf. There she is, beyond the broken wire fence, up and away towards the sloping limestone ridge.

He walks across the thick-grassed paddock, paspalum bending, applying its stickiness to trousers and socks. Thigh high. Belly high on a beast. Dammit, he sighs again. How did she get in there? The cow swings her head to watch Maitland wading towards her. There is a tremble in her limbs; a line of drool drips, hangs, drops from her jaw.

Maitland takes all afternoon to haul up the few strands of fence with the heavy wire-strainer. His mind feels fogged; his discontent sits in his gut.

'Why?' He asks Sarah again that evening. 'Why are you like this? I'm locked out. It's you and Lucy. Lucy and you. Why don't you touch me, even?'

Sarah's face wears a glazed look. Her eyes gaze into the distance, through him. He does not realize this is her defence. 'I have no strength,' she explains. 'I keep telling you. I can only look after Lucy. You're an adult, surely...'

'I have needs, too.'

'Between your legs!' She yells, suddenly angry. 'You're all drink and dick.'

'No,' Maitland says. 'It's not like that.' But Sarah has gone to her room, slamming doors.

Fuck you, Sarah. Anger and defeat compress his lips and Maitland's hands fist deep into his gritty pockets.

For a while, the cows had bunched against the fence, walking its length. Now they are quiet in their safe paddock on the far side of the uncertain ridge.

Maitland rides across to check, paspalum covers the horse's flanks and legs with its dark ergot, making the dog bounce and leap, the small black specks sticking to its fur. And finds Maybellene deep in the darkly seeded paddock. 'Cheers Maybellene,' he grins, raising his flask to her. 'You're not looking for your bloody calf, are you? You're into this stuff.' And he waves his arm, its arc encompassing the field. Maybellene, nodding, rocks on unsteady legs.

That evening, just before dark, he finds the house-paddock empty again. Can she die of it? Should've read the book.

He can see Maybellene up on the ridge like a great bone-angled statue, silhouetted against the sky, close by the ancient tree. 'Don't go there, you crazy cow…go back. Maybellene!' And Maitland half runs, half scrambles across the uneven ground, trips and hauls himself up again, flailing to keep his balance in this drunken race. Baffled at his erratic progress towards her, Maybellene swings her dull head, loses her footing, props sideways, vanishes.

'Jesus!' Maitland's boot catches the top of a secret stone and he hurtles forward, clutching at nothing.

From where he is lying, Maitland can see a grey triangle of sky, latticed with branches and leaves of the gnarly tree. From the colour of the sky, he thinks it is morning. Or evening? His head aches from the impact. Beneath his chilled fingers, he encounters rock and twiggy dirt, and then softness, warmth and a heavy breathing. Oh, God. The word sighs from his lips. Oh, Maybellene. And he remembers. He has slithered bumped dropped somehow to the bottom of this hole, where he lies on his back beside a stunned cow.

Minutely, he flexes his body. Thighs. Toes. Shoulders and arms. Everything works. His fingers seek the soreness on his head and he sees a smear of blood, feels the dampness in his hair. Passing giddiness sweeps his vision into odd angles that he cannot shake away. Kneeling, he strokes the cow, runs ignorant hands over her body, across the wide curved ribs beneath the satiny skin and along the strong and knocky legs. But Maybellene lies there.

'You'll be all right,' he tells the cow, and at the sound of his voice, she tries to rise, but falls back again, a deep, fathomless noise sounding in her throat.

In the almost-dark, he edges around the wall, ripping his nails on useless cracks and clefts. He reaches as high as he can but there's nothing to grip and the tiny ledges where he might have put a boot tip, are too tiny. He needs a rope, but such things are far away, down in the shed near the house where the woman sits alone by a cradle.

A smile softens her lips, smooths her frown, as she tucks the shawl around her small likeness. Snoozes.

Lavender's blue, diddle diddle, rosemary's green, when I am king, diddle diddle, you shall be queen…

Shey Saint-Malo

Thalasso

A voice from darkness damps the air, so heavy. So heavy, impossible to move, his body flattened upon the tiles, as if it no longer belongs to him. A shiver leaves a sense of being naked and exposed. Attempts to touch anything fail, unable to engage his fingers. Hands and feet anchored to the floor, the tongues sink down to him in language both foreign and familiar. Insistent, urgent tones compel him now to open his eyes. Glare from the hot lights above obscures their faces but not their naked bodies. A dozen or more men encircle him, heads bent, peering down into his face. Two of them reach out and, still paralysed, he is rising up to meet them.

After the nauseating ride from steam to ice, they meet amid the thaw, at first in parallel. Flash of white robe, the squelching of rubber soles on tile, smudged scent of mud and algae. She is transposed about him, at once ahead, beside and behind. Vague syllables escape from him then evaporate leaving only a minute vibration on his lips, to which she returns a smile-frown. Pixilated light and space settle on him like dust and then burrow under his skin. Numbness of flesh and thought, and a tingling without origin suspended somewhere, perhaps only in memory. He pinches a chunk of frozen forearm between his fingernails and squeezes and squeezes. Nothing hurts. Nothing but benign indentations which could turn out to be cuts when the blood returns.

During the rewarming, breath snagged on lingering chlorine, taut stretching of skin across cheekbone, he finds it easier to listen than speak. Watching her lips move and hearing the sound emerge a split second too late as if they were part of an old film fallen into asynchrony, the feeling is that of a different time, a different place. Her speech forms a meandering harmonic behind the veil of tinnitus. Echoes from the naked men in the adjacent thalassotherapy room take flight, his name a chorus in the reverberation on the walls. He stumbles over feet three sizes too large in an effort to hurry out of hearing range, and she steadies him by the arm. Gradually, her fingertips seer a flush of revival back into his opalescent skin, warmth diffusing from elbow to shoulder and beyond.

Inside the massage room, a scent of cinnamon and frankincense and a view of the North Sea create a dual effect, simultaneously warm and cold. Finally, the coffee she places between his hands catalyses the thawing until all the layers of sound converge into one and now they too can exist together in the same moment. Her voice is calm, if clipped, as she tells him not to worry, that these things happen regularly with first-timers. They fail to take into consideration sudden changes in temperature on the body – the shock of the ice pool after the sauna. He realises now that the warnings were all there, he just wasn't looking for them. A mismatch of habit and initiation.

Under a blue lamp, he allows the last fragment of robe to leave his fists, sounds of Schubert in the background. Face down, eyes closed, hot spiced oil running into the small of his back, he replays in his mind that Baltic winter steaming.

Second time around, he knows the pattern for complacency is set within the cedar walls, the eucalyptus carried on a warm vapour. Its smoky familiarity, reassuring yet deceptive, close up and whisper hoarse.

Thoughts drift to mirage afternoons on Scarborough Beach and the salty, sticky heat in his hair, essence of ghost gum and pine carried to the shoreline on a hot easterly. Bodies, colour coded in batches according to frequency of visit, daub the sandscape. When the temperature reaches the limit for tolerance, the multi-hued forms rise and disappear into shimmering blue.

In here, though, they are all a variation on a theme of pasty white. Occasionally, a shifting figure or involuntary twitch catches his attention but immediately he diverts his gaze from the pack. Someone in the far corner is snoring amongst a collective humid hibernation, each one in their own safe place and decorated with beads of melting waste. Having reached his limit, dizzy, drowning in sodden air, he hurries out the door and heads towards a cool place.

Diving into shimmering blue, ten degrees and razor sharp against skin, lungs constricting beneath spasmed ribs, he is sinking into darkness.

Gail Willems

Tripped Out

I
on a cycle of argentine she wheeled her way
sunwise winewise head lost in blue
flew on roads of fortune made worlds shiver
wedged her way through the prism gates
fingered rubies out of a pomegranate
cradled the needle in her arm all night

as skin dissembled in peppermint light
butterflies swam their wings in her veins
toenails and fingernails crazed
she cradled the needle in her arm all night

II
under streetlights tangled on corners
children played football pointed their feet away   a busker
mixed footprints in her dust   the weight of her body
leaked into the shadows   a ballad of bones
strummed silence on a sleazy wall
too young to wash up on a bitter street
a needle cradled in her arm all night

III
I bring you this patchwork its threads slipping
dissolving   nothing left to hold
never again to hear her mother's voice
or the vibration of guitar strings
through the white fizz of time
does someone remember her eyes
hug her shadow the needle cradled in her arm

was she simply a cancelled dream

Helga Jermy

Second Skin

I felt that slip before, as we were herded
into the cattle barn departure lounge of
St Petersburg, then Leningrad, and they
said you looked like Pushkin and they took you
off for questioning and a search through
souvenirs, and I felt the icy fear of the gulags,
fury for the lost ten years of my vanavanemad
held captive in the desolate bear hug of Siberia,
and you returned and slipped me back, laughed
at the quaintness of their paranoia, drank
tea from their samovars and I smiled behind a
mask as they stamped and displayed their armoury.

I slipped before as a tear let show the squeaky
shed skin of Taat's isamaa, new cultural cloak
a flimsy guise, pinned scarred grieved.
I zip my skin, this thorny raw hide, this gabardine
against cold war and distant rain, until my skin
begins to itch again or the hungry growl of
the bear creeps back into my dreams.

Translation from Estonian
Vanavanemad = grandparents
Taat = dad/father
Isamaa = fatherland

Sophie Curzon-Siggers

selkie child

i.
maybe she was pulled
too soon
from the inland sea –

submerged
ten months
resisting pleas,
exorcising February heat
and vindaloo.

maybe forceps
were the spirit
snagging
trauma
of netting
beyond consciousness.

ii.
ridged extremities
are swimming's
reproach:
but she appears
still forming

salt-rubbed, her skin
mere underlay
to foam neoprene;

her eyes enduringly
without horizon,
stem cell
rock pools.

iii.
maybe it is our ancestry
in this coastal town,
something
in the water.

opinions, medical
and otherwise
sought or unsolicited:

let her swim 24/7
she'll tire of it
soon enough

(but even seal lions
sleep, overlapped
as summer foliage
on the rock commune.
nightly the reenactment
her bed hosts,
toy seals prop
her head and limbs);

you're enablers –
cut off the supply,
give her normal
child interests

(salt water withdrawal,
her prone form
in grass, a dark cut
of seaweed, self consoling
with intermittent southerly
breeze.)

iv.
our fridge calendar lacks
extra-curriculars – booked out
by shoreline vigils,
private lifeguard shifts.
her drowning impossible
we supervise innate
attraction, corporeal vocation

the undertow indiscriminately conducted
by water, air, earth
corralling her
to the sea lion colony.

vi.
in the hall cavity
a chronology of wetsuits, outgrown
selkie skins
archived in sanctity, more
organic than
baby teeth.

when lock-down begins
at dusk's hour of enlivenment
she retreats there,

gazing at
ebony origami
sculpted for her
in cave dim.
tonight she allowed
me, and folded
limbs into the observatory.

we are underwater
contemplating
the surface from
beneath.

Flora Smith

Swan River Colonist

Lulled by the heat and by the rhythmic dip of oars
she fought the body's wish to slide sleepwards.
Sloth must not hold sway when everything is new.

I do not know these trees, yet the grey bushes part
when we come close and here are giants! Cream trunks
with such markings! Scribblings and painted patches of red,
brown, cream. I do not know these trees, but I might love them.

Black swans sailed unperturbed downstream,
smaller birds sped past before her eyes could measure
or observe. Now a raucous chorus came from treetops –
large brown birds confident in their cacophany.

The swans are beautiful but they are not white
and are there many birds that shriek and do not sing?
This lash of light that blinds me when I raise my eyes –
must it always chase away the clouds?
Will it be always so, this otherness of things?

She gazed at her father, at the silver buttons glinting
at his cuffs as he rowed, and she remembered he had said:
We must expect it will be difficult and different.

And the fact that he had said so, and so it was,
lent calm acceptance to his observant daughter, who sat upright
in hat and gloves and looked about her while the others slept.

Rebecca Raisin

Shades of Sienna

It was a Tuesday.

I woke late that morning. Burdened, by a restless night of murky dreams filled with nebulous warnings. Or did I just imagine it in my somnambulist haze? I felt like I'd pressed the shiny silver snooze button two hundred and eighty eight times, and I was not prone to exaggeration.

It was unusual, I never slept late. I was one of those crazy morning people. My usual catch cry to the non-believers was: the early bird catches the worm. Let's make haste. Things have since changed.

I felt groggy, seasick. Enveloped by a grey mist that I couldn't shake.

Sienna and I had plans. We were going to my sister-in-law's house to make a photo collage for my brother's surprise fortieth birthday. I was taking my photo evidence to merge with hers, of his mighty presence in all of our lives.

I showered quickly, feeling claustrophobic in the small recess, the steam too similar to the fog that had suffocated my sleep. I dressed for comfort. Black tracksuit, dark blue sneakers. Hair up, not a scrap of make-up. Almost like I wanted to be invisible.

I padded down the small hallway to Sienna's room. Waves of guilt washed over me for making her wait like that. Sienna was not like other five years olds. She would not leave her room without me. Something in her labyrinth of a mind would not allow it. I had to cross that threshold and guide her out. Holding her left hand.

I opened her door softly, my eyes pleading forgiveness. There she sat, on her perfectly made bed. Hair brushed, dressed, hands clasped in her lap.

'*Sorry*, sorry, baby, that I made you wait,' I walked into the room and breathed her in. Fresh like lemons. She was my lifeline, I only felt complete when I could see her, touch her, feel her. She was the last piece of the jigsaw.

She gazed at me lovingly, and again my heart caught at the sheer wonder of her. Sienna's eyes were the colour of the ocean. The two colours of the ocean. One eye the translucent topaz blue you wade through, and the other eye the teal green that disguises the rip.

I embraced her. We were like magnets, drawn together by an invisible force. I held her left hand and walked across the threshold. Another remarkable thing about Sienna was her silence. She wasn't vocal. She had never cried as a baby, never babbled. Never, ever uttered a word.

I always thought because of these differences she was somehow more, though by others she was seen as less. Another sign, another marker. *Something's not right*, they said.

We drove in silence, which I remember unsettled me. The radio frequency hurt my ears, like they were suddenly super-sensitive. Sienna locked eyes with me in the rear view mirror and did not move them for the rest of the drive. She was drinking me in. I began to make silly conversation, my voice sounding too high and slightly manic.

After what felt like days, we pulled into the busy street my sister-in-law lived on. Her ground floor apartment was directly across from the South Perth foreshore, which cancelled out the fact that she had hordes of traffic whizzing by most of the day. She said they just looked 'over' the cars to the deep water beyond.

Usually we had to park a block away but that day, at that moment, I thought luck had shone down on me; there, right out the front of their apartment, was a single car space, meant for me. Sienna and I grabbed our bags and books.

I remember again, inhaling Sienna's citrus smell as my sister-in-law opened the door before I had a chance to knock.

'You look tired?' She said it as a question.

'Yeah, weird night of bad dreams.'

'Are you okay? What happened to you yesterday?'

'What do you mean?'

'You were meant to come here yesterday.'

'No, it was always today. Tuesday. Maybe we misunderstood each other.'

'Today is Wednesday.'

The stench of ammonia hit me. A quick whiff of poison.

What happened to Tuesday?

We crossed the threshold. I organised Sienna at the dining room table with her colouring books and pencils. Took out her yellow drink bottle. She was happy on her own. My sister-in-law walked from the kitchenette with a pot of tea and some cups. Concern etched on her face.

'Are you up to this?' she asked.

'Of course, looking at photos, it's not exactly *taxing*.'

'Well, if you're sure. Let's sit on the front porch.'

We ambled out. Her with the tea and me with my photo albums.

There was still a chill to the air, even though the sun was out. It glinted off the ripples of the water, making me squint.

We sat on the love swing they'd had forever. It was deep ruby red and had been re-upholstered twice since they had lived here. The elements ravaged it, but they kept rejuvenating it. It was an indelible part of them.

The swaying swing had a calming effect on me. The cool of the breeze on my skin washed away the remnants of confusion I felt.

My sister-in-law pushed with pale pink toes the faded wood of the deck each time the swing drew forward. She blew on the hot tea before sipping.

I opened one of the albums. It was a dusty rose colour and had baby rattle decals glued haphazardly over the cover. I remembered making it, just after Sienna was born. Trying my new scrapbooking skills, while she slept the sleep of angels.

My sister-in-law's mobile rang from inside. She put her tea down and walked in to answer it. I could hear her garbled voice, droning, like the sound of a thousand bees underwater.

I looked down at the pink album, the first page was blank.

I turned to the next page. Blank.

I frowned. I could see traces of glue, where my photos had been. The paper was discoloured where chemicals had infected the fibre.

I kept turning page after page of blankness.

I bit down on the panic I felt. Surely they had fallen out in the car?

I closed the album, averting my eyes from my hands so I didn't see the slight quake in them. My sister-in-law walked back out, her shoulder cradling the phone. She looked at me, mouthed a silent apology and continued discussing prices with someone. She was a freelance photographer who mainly worked on location but had a small studio in one of the spare bedrooms inside.

She sat back down on the swing, realising this wasn't going to be a brief conversation. She rolled her eyes at me signalling the caller's need to question, as she explained the merits of various locations for timeless wedding photos.

I tapped her jean-clad leg and pointed to my car, I wanted to find the missing photos. I started to doubt my memory; maybe I had three albums? Did I re-do the scrappy scrap-booking one?

My sister-in-law nodded. I walked down the small patch of grass. I doubt I was even a metre away when I heard her. It was like a slow motion movie sequence. I saw my arm outstretched, reaching for the door handle. My other hand, thumb still on the unlock button on my remote.

I heard her without seeing her. I knew it was her voice. 'Mummy, don't move.'

I heard the sharp intake of my breath next. It almost winded me, I stood, frozen. She spoke? Where was she? It sounded like she was right beside me. I whipped my head around, looking for those eyes, the comfort of them.

My sister-in-law looked like a parody. The phone flew from her hands, bounced once on the deck before resting on the grass. Red 'on' button flashing. Her expression changed to horror. It looked like she was screaming, but I couldn't hear her. Her hands flew to her face, to shield her, protect her from what she might witness.

I was facing the apartment now. I could see my reflection in the silver double glazed windows. The effect was like mirrors from a fun house, everything seemed wider, rippled, distorted; like a caricature. I saw the flash of red metal in the reflection, bubbling like crimson waves rushing toward me. My sister-in-law looked like she was doggy paddling upside down, hands like scoops, beckoning urgently. To me?

I grabbed at my ears. The high pitched frequency had returned. It felt as though someone was slicing through my brain with an angle-grinder. Time moved back into its frenetic pace, trying impossibly to catch up on the slowing. I heard her again: 'Mummy, get down.'

This time I just listened. I fell to the ground, still with my hands covering my ears. My eyes closed, face crushing soft blades of cold grass. The sound of metal crunching, crashing, folding, wiped out my numbness. Hysteria is volume, so loud; it must be what hell sounds like.

I could smell fear; it was ammonia again. A shadow flew across me as my car was airborne, just missing me. My hair flew up in the slipstream, as I buried my face further into the blades.

I could hear my sister-in-law scream, fraught with anguish, knowing it was for me. Maybe she thought I was under the car, that I was gone, in an instant; just like that. I hoped Sienna wasn't close. The sound stopped, as I felt red.

I awoke to an annoying beep. I reached my hand out to silence the alarm. Five more minutes. If I could just find the shiny silver snooze button. I touched air. Opened my eyes to a too bright room. Saw tubes, wires, machines, starch faced nurses. Closed my eyes. Remembered.

Heard my sister-in-law like she had taken up residence in my ear. 'She's awake. I felt her left hand move. She's awake!'

Heard running footsteps, stampeding toward me. My brother, his face zoomed in over mine, his eyes probing mine, like he didn't believe I was there.

I blinked a few times. They smiled.

'See, she's back,' my sister-in-law said.

I looked around the room. Dizziness overwhelmed me. I felt waves of nausea. I was adrift. I closed my eyes, worked up the energy to look around again. Took a deep breath. *Oh god, was that ammonia again?*

My eyes open, now frantically seeking her out.

Where was she?

'Where's Sienna?' I asked them.

They looked at each other, puzzled.

'Who?' My brother asked.

It's been two years since the accident and I still think of her every day. I still see her. You know the feeling someone is standing behind you, and you turn but you're never quite quick enough to catch a glimpse of them?

Debbie Stephan

Inside Knowledge

'How would you like me to sit?'

'There are various options. But let's just talk a little first. Tell me about your interests. Are you a sporting man?'

'I used to play squash but now it's more often golf. Less strenuous. Not doing too badly there.'

'Other interests? You have beautiful bone structure. Could you turn your face a little to the left? Yes, the shadow down your temple and beneath your cheekbone is extraordinary. Could you take your glasses off?'

'I only need them for reading so there is no necessity for me to wear them.'

'Possibly discarded on the desk near your hand? What are your other interests?'

'Well, there is the yacht – I sail whenever I can.'

'So a coastal scene behind you? What else?' The older man hesitated as his phone began to vibrate. On checking the screen he replied, 'Excuse me. I have to take this' and took several paces towards the door before he continued, 'Raise the bid to $2.65. No more than $2.67. I don't think they'll hold out beyond that…Yes, Jeans Right…ripe for the pickings, absolutely…no, no doubt…good, I'll be back in an hour. Have it ready for me then. Cheers'. Then turning back to me, he continued, 'Now, where were we? Seated by a desk? I think that sounds about right. How many sittings will this take?'

The commission had come to me as most corporate commissions did, via the Archibald. Every year I submitted two or three paintings, without any expectation of winning – my style was far too traditional for that – but with the expectation of having at least one painting hung. This was what I needed for the corporate work to come in. In general, corporate clients much preferred a recognisable likeness to an artistic interpretation and this I delivered in spades. The current sittings were with the head of Beystone Holdings, Martin Jaeger, a man who had achieved phenomenal growth for his company over the past three years.

While my style is traditional, my passion is to emulate the techniques of the old masters. I had been experimenting with adding chalk to hand-mixed pigments, achieving both body and translucency in the finished result. But my recent experiments were with raw linseed oil: with sun-thickened oil I was achieving the glazing effects of enamel-like finishes but with burnt plate oil, especially in combination with chalk, I was beginning to discover a wide range of impasto effects, reminiscent of the seventeenth-century masters. So, while I was beginning to make real progress with glazing and impasto, progress was both slow and expensive. Hence my current financial crisis, flowing directly from the global one which had reduced my commissions to a trickle.

After Jaeger had left and I had cleaned up the studio for the day, I turned on the computer to check my emails – GalleryOne advising of a sale and several bills, with the bills outweighing the sale by three to one. With the rent on the studio also due shortly, I was rapidly losing ground and badly needed another source of income to stay afloat. And that was when I had the idea. I looked up the share price for Jeans Right – $2.24 at close of business but expected to rise, according to several reports in the financial pages over the past week.

The following day, the reports were even more favourable and the share price had jumped by another two cents. I was desperate. My work needed my full-time devotion to the experiments with pigments and oils, documented meticulously in a series of forty-six notebooks. And surely this chance was one in a million – all that was seemingly required of me was the courage to jump. Without further thought, I put in a bid for all the savings I had – $9000 worth of Jeans Right stock – and shut down the computer, as if to close the matter.

But I was distracted and could think of nothing else. My concentration was shot and, at my next sitting with Jaeger, I was edgy, hoping for more inside information. But it was not until the third sitting that I learnt more.

'Hope you don't mind if I leave the phone on this time?' asked Jaeger, 'I'm expecting some calls.'

'No, not a problem', I replied, attempting to sound as disinterested as possible, 'I can always carry on with the background if that occurs'. Sure enough, within ten minutes, Jaeger took a few steps away to take a call.

'Yes, we'll close it today…offer $2.69…I know they're holding out for more but that's it…close it today or we go public tomorrow AM and put it to their shareholders…No, COB today. Cheers.'

While my hands continued to paint the third glaze of shadow in shades of cobalt blue, my mind went into overdrive. Jeans Right shares were currently sitting at $2.30 and Jaeger was offering $2.69, a difference of 39 cents a share. Therefore another $25,000 worth of stock today, could mean a total profit of nearly $6000 on the sale price tomorrow. If I maxed out my credit card and delayed payment on the rent, I could just raise it.

As soon as the sitting was done I made the transaction then leaned back in my chair, feeling an overwhelming sense of relief that I had at last acted to save the studio and my work.

I slept more soundly that night than I had in months and was up early the following morning, to check the papers. The financial pages announced a bid by Beystone Holdings for Tasman Jeans at $2.69 a share. Hastily, I checked for other reports, groaning and dropping my head in my hands when I realised the reports were accurate. More and more of the story emerged over the next few days. Beystone Holdings had been courting both companies but had made the final bid for Tasman Jeans, on the back of their third-quarter profit result. And my shares had also taken a tumble, once Beystone's intentions were made public.

But every cloud also has a silver lining, I tell myself. I didn't go under, though it was a near thing until GalleryOne completed a fire sale on three of my landscapes. I completed Jaeger's portrait and it resulted in another commission from Beystone Holdings when the chairman of the board saw the finished product. Jaeger's portrait didn't turn out too badly either – the luminosity of the skin tones and the complex impasto effects were re-marked upon – and the painting was hung in the Archibald the following year, attracting a welcome flurry of new corporate work from those want-ing to emulate Jaeger's business successes.

Of course, I still have my Jeans Right stock, which has now bottomed out at $1.26 and I may eventually recoup my investment, or so my broker thinks. And yes, I have a broker, who advised on an investment in Beystone Holdings, which is doing very well at present and could even triple in the next year or two, or so my broker thinks.

Peter Rondel

The Ace of Spades

Somewhere out near Boulder there's a rusty spade. I mention it because it's significant in the history of the gold rush days. I'm probably one of the few who knows about it now. You could pass it a hundred times and never notice it there beside the old track. The blade is stuck in a large boulder, rather like the Excalibur, as my grandfather had described it. I've never tried to extract it and never would. It's the way it came to be stuck in that great piece of rock that makes it special. I came to know about it from my grandfather. It was his father, my great grandfather, who owned that old spade and the story that goes with it.

Back when Kalgoorlie was a thriving King Solomon's mine, so to speak, my great grandfather spent the last of his meagre savings on a few tools and enough stores to last about three months. He'd heard about the gold finds out there and decided to grab a piece of the fortune. Like so many others, he wasn't really prepared for the territory, the weather or the work. Oh, he did find gold, enough to fill his old snuff box, but it took months of digging to do it. He traded it in and bought more provisions then went back to his site. Each time he collected enough gold to do so, he went back to Boulder and sold it.

I first heard the story when I was twelve. My grandfather and my father were sitting on the verandah steps drinking beer. I knew it was rude to eavesdrop, but something that my father asked really caught my imagination. 'So, did he actually find any gold?'

Granddad took a long drink from his beer mug and laughed. 'Yep. Never more than you could hold in a matchbox, in fact he stored it all in an old snuffbox. That was the only thing left, that snuffbox – still got it to this day. If you want it, I'll bring it up next visit.'

'What about his wife? She never went out there?'

'Not on your life – too fond of discipline. She was influenced by Edith Cowan. She was a strong, no-nonsense woman, while he'd do anything for a laugh. I think Dad got fed up with her controlling ways and lack of humour. It came down to a choice of running off to sea or gold prospecting.

He used to get seasick so the gold was a better option. Paddy Hannan had struck gold out Kalgoorlie way and as always happens, things got exaggerated and tales of big gold strikes were attracting people from all over the place.'

'What did his wife have to say about it?'

'Nothing. She woke up one morning and he was gone. With me and my brother to raise; she wasn't too impressed. Her mood did improve a bit when Dad managed to send some small nuggets back to her. She took up teaching down in Fremantle to pay the bills.'

'So what became of him? I take it he never made his fortune?'

Granddad slowly stood up. 'Hang on, I've got something that should interest you.'

He went into the house and re-emerged with a cardboard cylinder. 'Take a look at this.'

My father slid a roll of paper out of the tube and unrolled it. 'It's a map.'

'That's the location of his old dig. It was registered at the local office and when it all happened, they sent it down to my mother. I don't think she even looked at it – just threw it into a drawer and left it there.'

'Have you ever tried to find it?'

'I did do once, a good few years ago. Took three days to find it; I only knew for certain that it was the right place when I found what was left of his hat, wedged in the fork of a tree. It still had his name inside on the hat-band.'

'Did you find anything else?' By then I had moved closer, disregarding the impropriety and trying not to be noticed. I didn't want to miss a word.

'That's the main part of this story. The actual dig is now just a hole in the ground about fifteen feet deep. It's overgrown with weed now. About fifty feet away is a group of big boulders, just sitting there like someone had dropped them there. Anyway, the biggest of them had a spade stuck in its side. Jammed in there forever I reckon, just like that Excalibur.'

'How did it come to be like that?'

'Well, after about three years, Dad started to get a bit troppo, you know, talked to himself all the time and never seemed to recognize anyone when he came in to Boulder – not even at the pub. Others recognized the signs but couldn't do much. I got the drum from an old feller in the pub there. He told me what happened.'

Granddad noticed me lying face down in the corner and waved a hand in the direction of the back yard. 'I think you should go and cut some fire wood down near the shed, young feller.'

I remember that day like it was yesterday. A big mob of cockies were flying from tree to tree and making a heck of a din. Dad seemed unusually intolerant and threw a stick up at them but they didn't seem to notice, in fact they made even more noise.

Granddad died a couple of weeks later. It seems that he knew that his visit that week was to be his last. It took me nearly twenty years to uncover the truth. I'd come across that old map and as the days passed, my curiosity got the better of me. Armed with the map and no idea of how I would find the site, I drove out to Kalgoorlie where I eventually did find it. It was several miles east of Boulder in an area now owned by a big mining company. There wasn't much to see, just a big hole in the ground that never led anywhere and that great boulder with the spade still stuck in it. The metal fitting that once held the handle was rusted away and the shaft was split and bleached white.

The registrar's office was open and smelled of antiquity; that old-wood smell that only comes with age. The wooden floor had worn to a hollow just inside the door and a well-worn track was trodden into it, leading to the counter. The computer seemed very much out of place on that old desk. The man who sat behind it looked up as I entered, staring at me through a very powerful pair of spectacles. He looked more like an undertaker and I surmised that back in those old days, he probably would have been.

'Can I help you?'

'I hope so. I'm researching my great grandfather's history. He once had a mine east of Boulder. I just want to know what happened to him.'

The man got up. He had something to take an interest in, at last. 'What was his name?' He moved to the computer and sat down.

'McLauchlan – Andrew McLauchlan. Eighteen ninety four I think.'

The clerk set the computer to search and stood up. 'Let's see what we can find.'

He seemed like a different man now, quite happy in fact. I heard him talking to himself as he sat down at the desk and read through the papers that the computer had produced. He took his time and grunted occasionally as he read. Eventually he stood up and handed me the papers. One page was of particular interest. It was a small article from the newspaper of the time. Great Granddad had chosen to follow in the footsteps of several other miners when he lost everything in a poker game. The hole in the ground at the old site was made when he sat on a case of dynamite and lit the fuse. It was that explosion that drove the spade into the rock and completely evaporated everything that had existed on that spot. I was shocked to learn that a number of miners were known to have done the same thing. Disappointment and loneliness eventually got too much for some and they chose that way to end it.

This then was the topic of conversation all those years ago, when I was banished from the scene and sent to chop firewood. Perhaps they were right, and the story may well have given me nightmares. I've got a large photo of that spade in the rock, in a frame on the wall; it's a great conversation starter.

Kelly Pilgrim-Byrne

Memories Are Our Truest Heirlooms

Solemn, she says
when asked how it felt to hold him.

Found under foot in the shallows of Coogee,
melding to her hand like a slow dancer
wrapping – curling, curling – wrapping,
inching as a thousand summers pass.

She asks to set him free to be with his family
and he slides through her fingers,
silently parachutes to the sea floor
settles, camouflaged by insipid yellows.

Starfish.

Janet Jackson

there

You want to know my deepest darkest
secret? Don't ask me at a table
of blithe people –
ask me with the walls up around us
and the doors locked.

My deepest darkest secret is
that I am a poet. Therefore
I am allowed no secrets
but to tell them I must make them
into art.

If you could see into my guts
you would find, not daffodils
in Grecian urns, not wet wheelbarrows
of chilly plums,
but the sun, the fusion forcing
the green fuse, juicing up
the portable panels
like the red sound
of a red guitar…

on the good days.
On the bad days you'd find, as black
as burnt bark
or tarmac
or a Melbourne coat
or a habit
or the dead face
of a dead laptop,
the hole
left by the nova,
a naked
singularity,
enigmatic as fuck,
with Stephen Hawking
and Paul Davies

orbiting it
uncertainly, books
clutched in their hands,
while Louis MacNeice
performs a comic dance,
Bono quotes Bukowski
to anyone who'll listen,
Martha Wainwright
curses her luck,
Ursula Le Guin
dreams of utopia
and Stephen Daedalus
leans on his ashplant,
wreathed in a terrible smile.

My deepest darkest secret is there
in the bridge of the song, the volta
of the poem. I put it there
to keep from it squatting
under my ribcage
giving me hell.

My deepest darkest
secret is that I
think most poems
are crude oil,
most paintings
are coal,
most music
is diesel smoke,
most of us,
as we carry on
with our carbon reactions,
our hot oxidations,
have no idea, are afraid
to find out, are afraid
to behold
how amazingly
beautiful, valuable, diamond-
facet clear, diamond-blade
useful,
yet graphite-pencil
erasable
we are.

Zan Ross

Historical Leathers

Where the conservative brown version was the lie
I accepted, pigs   might leap over the moon. Not so
impossible considering cows, *Hey, diddle diddle*,
I ran down the hill covered with daffodils/butter flowers:
Hold one up to your chin and it looks as if
the generals have to be the most chic – he was
waiting for me at the cottage in the Black Forest,
black boots vibrating floorboards, *blouson* tight
across his chest. How I loved the smell of his
leather jacket, coupled with khaki. Almost sliding
the elliptic of French Jewess, my hair feathering skin –
I would never do him when he was naked: *Clothes*
maketh the man. Gestapo coats and panzer
uniforms crowd racks on the day, posture
the platform at Auschwitz. *See*
the trenches, piles of detritus, rooms full of
hair. He stands, **black leather jacket regulation**
post-Patton image, the perfect host: hides me,
rides me in an upper room. I avoid becoming
a lampshade. *The dish ran away with the spoon*.
Later I witness *The Night Porter* **roaring post-war**
economy I've been saved for. It's why   retail
succeeded **immediately after World War II** –
Hey, diddle diddle. We're in this flesh-to-flesh,
ashes-to-ashes, profit commodity on a hill covered in
butter-flowers, his whip curled in one hand when I
touch the match to our clothes.   *The cow*
jumps over the moon.

Parts of this borrowed from Mick Farren's *The Black Leather Jacket*.

Ian C. Smith

Water Sports (for Jordan)

Near the finishing line, he sees them
a kilometer distant, on the screen
tiny silent detonations of water
rowing rhythmically in fifth place.

He recalls the two of them in the bath
the strange new job of house-husband
his belief that he had left sport behind
the boy's physical intensity.

The race caller's tone, tempo, quicken.
These brawny boys in dark glasses
are poised to challenge for third.
His own guttural cry surprises him.

Embarrassed, he quietens, unclenches
but his heart hammers with fight.
Urged hoarsely, they vie for second
or even better, a schoolboy dream.

They squirted, splashed, taking turns
catching each other full in the face
he overacting spluttering outrage
his young son shrieking in delight.

The shining boys' timing is golden.
His roar becomes a howl like feedback.
Water glitters, the coach's face pink
his crew's muscle swooned in ecstasy.

Ending the game honorably was difficult
floor flooded, the bath now at low tide
water dripping, the two of them spent
the boy wanting to keep going, to win.

Jan Napier

Childhood Diabetes

Snail shell spirals draw down the eye
prick colour's centre
my clever girl licks at a future
soon to fade and lose its brightness
a lifeline smiled in lollipops
dizzy pinks   urine yellows
treats to keep her forever young
in this place of no sweetness.
Too few years skip into the sucker's
concentric circles.

Ruth Stubbings

Delores

EXT. FARMHOUSE - DAWN

Rain pours and lightning blazes across the dawn sky.

A MAN drenched in mud drags the body of a dead PROSTITUTE through overgrown grass toward a decrepit farmhouse set back from the black, deserted road.

The man is BOB, a forty-something trucker, hairy and tattooed from head to toe, pale face and hands stained with blood, so fat he struggles to breathe, or move. He seems distressed, constantly cursing himself under his breath and hitting his head with anger.

INT. FARMHOUSE LIVING ROOM - DAWN

JANEY (40) paces back and forth in a dowdy dressing gown, her hair unkempt, her face twisted in exhaustion, anxiously puffing on a cigarette.

Suddenly, she freezes and glares at the front door expectantly, cries.

EXT. FARMHOUSE - DAWN

Bob tosses the prostitute to the ground, refusing to look at her as he grabs a shovel sitting up against the house. He takes a deep breath and pounds the shovel into the damp earth, trying hard to be quiet as he digs the hole.

Suddenly, Janey emerges from the house. She looks down at the body and shakes her head, covering her face with distress at the sight.

                    JANEY
          You promised. You promised me.

Bob, caught red-handed, stands in front of the prostitute, trying to obstruct Janey's view of her. He bows his head.

                    BOB
          I ran out of time.

He glares up at the brightening sky and cringes.

                    JANEY (sighs)
          I'll do it. You get inside.

                    BOB
          No, Janey.

Janey takes the shovel from Bob's hand and kisses his cheek.

                    JANEY
          I'm not gonna let you die out here.

INT/EXT. FARMHOUSE - DELORES' BEDROOM - DAWN

DELORES (12) is tucked in tightly under the sheets of her bed. Her eyes widen with alarm as she listens to her father, Bob, drag his feet through the house and into his bedroom, slamming the door shut behind him.

                    DELORES
                   (whispers)
          Daddy...

She climbs out of her bed and leaps to the door, yanking on the handle, but it won't open. She groans with frustration, then walks to the window, discreetly peering out of it.

Outside she can see Janey digging a hole in the yard, sobbing and rubbing her face in between digs.

Delores gasps and falls back against her bed. She pulls the blanket over her head and grabs a flashlight and comic book from under her mattress, skims through the pages.

The comic book is based on Bram Stoker's Dracula. Delores gasps and groans as she sees the various images of Dracula biting necks and Van Helsing staking vampires.

> DELORES
> (gasps)
> Nosferatu.

EXT. FARMHOUSE - MORNING

Delores sways on a makeshift swing made from an old tyre and some rope hanging from a tree in the yard. She hums a haunting tune to herself as the wind helps to swing her back and forth.

Janey watches her from the kitchen window as she washes some dishes in the sink.

> JANEY
> Be careful, honey.

Delores smiles at her, then she stares over at the fresh grave, clumsily covered with moist earth and flowers.

She looks back at the kitchen window, checking if Janey is still watching, then slips off the tyre and cautiously walks to the grave.

She kneels down and runs her fingers over the mud and flowers, accidentally pricking her finger on a rose thorn. She gasps and brings her bleeding finger to her mouth.

> JANEY (CONT'D)
> Delores! You get away from there!

Delores jumps back with a fright.

> JANEY (CONT'D)
> Come help me with breakfast.

                    DELORES
        Aw. Do I have to?

                    JANEY
        Yes.

Delores frowns, crosses her arms and stomps her feet into
the house.

INT. FARMHOUSE KITCHEN - MORNING

Delores sits at the kitchen table intensely watching Janey
as she prepares their scrambled egg breakfast.

                    JANEY
        What is it, hon?

                    DELORES
        Is daddy home for good?

                    JANEY
        No, honey. You know that.

Delores looks down at her feet, sad.

                    DELORES
        Can I go see him?

Janey sits the scrambled eggs and toast in front of Delores.

                    JANEY

        No, darlin'. He'll come out when he's ready.

Delores stares down at the scrambled eggs with disgust and
blocks her nose. She pushes the plate away.

                    JANEY (CONT'D)
        Delores, you eat that.

She shakes her head defiantly and grabs an apple from the
fruit basket in the centre of the table. She takes a bite.

Janey sighs with surrender. She grabs the basket of washing from the table and languidly walks out to the yard with it.

INT. FARMHOUSE MASTER BEDROOM - MORNING

The room is in complete darkness. It is still and silent until three gentle knocks shatter the calm. Then:

> DELORES (O.S)
> (meekly)
>> Daddy...

No answer. The door creaks open. Light showers the room.

Delores stands in the doorway. She hesitates, then walks to the bed and kneels down, peering under it.

> DELORES (CONT'D)
>> Daddy...

Under the bed Bob sleeps flat on his back. He does not breathe. He does not move. He appears dead.

Delores climbs under the bed and reaches for his face.

Suddenly, Bob's eyes flash open with fright. He glares at her. He growls:

> BOB
>> Stay away...

She jolts back, then looks down at her bloodstained finger.

> DELORES
>> I cut my finger.

Bob screams, so loud it almost shatters the windows. He tosses the bed back, then grabs Delores and throws her against the door, knocking it off its hinges.
Janey charges into the room and screams at the sight of Delores dazed on the floor and Bob hovering over her with fangs protruding, his eyes glazed over with lust.

                    JANEY (screams)
        What are you doing?

Janey pulls Delores up into her arms and races out.

EXT. FARMHOUSE - MORNING

Janey runs out of the house with Delores in her arms and
collapses against the car. She pushes Delores into the
passenger seat, then runs around to the Driver's side and
climbs in.

Bob tumbles out the door and falls to his knees on the
stairs, cowering from the sun.

                        BOB
        Janey, please! I'm sorry!

Janey starts up the car and speeds toward the farm gates.

Bob chases after them, the sun hitting his skin and burning it instantly.

INT/EXT. CAR - MORNING

Janey screams as the car smashes into the farm gates.

Delores looks back at her father chasing the car, smoke
rising from his skin as it turns to flames.

                      DELORES
                     (screams)
        Daddy!

Janey looks at Bob through the rearview mirror. She gasps.

                       JANEY
              (turning Delores' face away)
        Don't look back, sweetie.

Delores cries. She grabs the blanket from the backseat,
then climbs out of the car and runs to Bob.

                        JANEY (CONT'D)
        Delores!

EXT. FARMHOUSE - MORNING

Delores throws the blanket over Bob's burning body and pats
at his skin, extinguishing the flames.

                        DELORES
            You have to get up, daddy. You have to
            get out of the sun.

Trembling from the pain, Bob struggles as he climbs up on
to his feet and staggers toward the house.

INT. FARMHOUSE MASTER BEDROOM - MORNING

Bob stumbles into his bedroom and collapses on the floor.
He trembles and moans from the pain as Delores loiters in
the background, not knowing what to do for her father.

                        BOB
            Delores, baby, I need you to leave me
            here and go make sure your mother is
            alright.

                        DELORES
                    (kneels beside him)
            But you need help.

Bob suddenly roars and covers his ears as though trying to
block out a loud, painful sound.

                        BOB
            Delores, you need to go.

Delores backs away, crying.

                        BOB (CONT'D)
                    (roars)
            Go!

She turns and runs.

EXT. FARMHOUSE - MORNING

Delores races out of the house to find Janey slumped on the stairs, despondent, broken. She falls beside her and throws her arms around her, sobbing and sobbing against her chest.

                    JANEY

     (rocking back and forth) Shh. Shh.

                    DELORES
          Will daddy die if he gets no blood?

Janey glares at her in shock.

                    JANEY
          He'll be alright until dark. For now we
          stay out here where it's safe.

Janey stands and gently ushers Delores over to the couch in the corner of the veranda where they rest.

                              DISSOLVE TO:

EXT. FARMHOUSE - TWILIGHT

Delores and Janey sleep on the couch as flies and mosqui-toes flutter around them. The mosquitoes keep biting De-lores' skin, leaving her in a rash of bites. She scratches and moans, then she opens her eyes to see--

--the prostitute standing before her, covered in dirt and mud, her hair matted with blood and earth, her throat torn. She stares down at Delores with lust, lips trembling, fangs out.

Delores screams and the prostitute lunges at her, but Janey wakes and slams a fist into the woman's face, knocking her off the veranda.

                    JANEY
          Get inside Delores!

Delores and Janey run for the door, but the prostitute flies up the stairs and grabs Janey by her hair, yanking her back into her arms, locking her to her chest as she savagely bites into her neck and tears her throat out.

> DELORES
> Mummy!

The prostitute drops Janey to the ground, glares at Delores, then runs for the farm gates and slams through them with such inhuman speed she becomes a blur.

Delores just stands there glaring down at her mother's mauled body in shock.

Then, she screams and races into the house.

INT. FARMHOUSE - MASTER BEDROOM - TWILIGHT

Delores collapses through the door and lands at Bob's side.

> DELORES
> (cries)
> Daddy... Daddy...

Bob is near death, his skin shriveled, his eyes sunken, unable to move or speak, a veritable corpse. He attempts to reach out for his daughter, but the effort is too much.

Delores takes hold of his hand and brings it to her cheek, then to her neck, making him feel her pulse. She cries.

> BOB
> (rasps)
> No...

He pulls his hand free from her and attempts to roll over on to his side, but he is too weak.

Delores lays down beside him, hugs him tight, then pushes her wrist to his mouth. He turns his head away, cries.

                         DELORES
          It's alright, daddy...

He looks at her despairingly, hesitates, then grabs her
wrist and bites her.

She cringes and looks away as tears escape her eyes.

INT/EXT. TRUCK - NIGHT

Bob drives the truck down a near-empty highway, singing
along to AC/DC blaring from the radio. He has a huge smile
on his face and he looks healthy with his radiant skin and
stunning bright blue eyes.

Delores sits beside him, also smiling and singing along
to the music. Her appearance is different, more startling:
hair thicker and lustrous, eyes hinging on a silver-blue,
and skin so translucent you could see your reflection in
it.

                         BOB
          Well, what do we have here?

Bob looks out his window and sees DYLAN (15) walking alongside the road with his thumb out, hitching for a ride.

Delores, excited by the sight of him, grips the dashboard.

                         DELORES
          Oh, please pick him up, daddy.

                         BOB
                       (laughs)
          Alright, alright.

He turns the truck around and drives up alongside the boy.

                      BOB (CONT'D)
          You alright, son?

Dylan slows his pace, looks up at Bob beneath the hood of
his jumper.

                    BOB (CONT'D)

It's a little late and you're a little
young to be out by yourself, don't you
think?

Dylan, glaring up at him, suddenly backs away, alarmed.

                    BOB (CONT'D)

Aw, don't worry about my skin, mate. I'm
part albino.

Delores giggles into her hands.

                    BOB (CONT'D)

So, you need a lift home or something?

Dylan nods his head.

                    BOB (CONT'D)
         What's your name?

                    DYLAN
         Dylan. What's yours?

                    BOB
         Bob. And this is my daughter Lola.

Delores leans forward and waves exuberantly at Dylan.

                    BOB (CONT'D)
         So, you want a lift?

Dylan, appearing nervous, gulps, nods his head.

                    DYLAN
         Thank you.

Bob jumps out of the truck and gestures for Dylan to climb
in.

Dylan hesitates. He looks up at Delores, then back to Bob.

                    BOB
                 (laughs)
      We don't bite, mate.

Dylan glares at him in shock, shakes his head, laughs.

                   DYLAN
              (under his breath)
         Yeah, right.

                    BOB
      What's that?

Suddenly, Dylan pulls a wooden stake from beneath his jumper and plunges it into Bob's chest and through his heart.

Delores screams and hurls herself at Dylan, but he hits her
off, yanks the stake from Bob's chest, and pushes her to
the ground, threatening to stake her with it as she cries
out:

                  DELORES
         My daddy... My daddy...

He hesitates, staring down at her as tears flood her eyes.
He curses under his breath, throws the stake away, then
stands up, backing away from her, ready for an attack.

                   DYLAN
         I'm sorry.

She flies up on to her feet and walks toward him.

                DYLAN (CONT'D)
      Your father turned my mother into a monster.

He opens the locket on his chest and inside it is a picture
of the prostitute.

                DYLAN (CONT'D)
         I had to kill her.

Delores reaches out for him and grabs his hand. He tries to
pull his hand free, but her hold is firm.

108

                    DYLAN (CONT'D)
        What do you want?

Delores wipes her tears away, then she smiles at him from
ear to ear, her fangs shining bright in the moonlight.

Dylan, understanding her intentions, shakes his head and
looks down at the stake.

Then, Delores growls and goes for his throat as we--

SMASH TO BLACK.

Notes on Contributors

Australian born **Richard James ALLEN** has published nine books as a poet, fiction and performance writer and editor, most recently *The Kamikaze Mind* (Brandl & Schlesinger). His writing has appeared widely in magazines, journals and anthologies, and online at the *Australian Poetry Library* and in *Second Life*. Dr Allen has combined a unique international career as a multi-award-winning poet, performer, choreographer, film and new media maker, and scholar, with screen adaptations of his writing at over 200 international film festivals as well as on television around the world, and live readings and performance adaptations at over 100 venues on three continents. Website: www.physicaltv.com.

Andrew BIFIELD is an expatriate Western Australian living in Melbourne. He won the inaugural 2012 Written Word category of the QANTAS Spirit of Youth Awards with a collection of poetry, and publishes short essays at www.andrewbifield.blogspot.com.au. He is currently working on a comic novel, provisionally entitled *Tacos at Midnight*.

Andrew BURKE has worn many masks throughout life – but he has always been a writer at heart. He is a failed drummer, a failed copywriter, a failed alcoholic, an amateur but failed drug addict, etc – all the disguises a creative person in our late capitalist society must wear to survive among the pedestrian hordes. Current poetry titles include *Undercover of Lightness* (Walleah Press, 2012, Hobart), *Shikibu Shuffle* with Phil Hall (above/ground press, 2012, Canada), and *QWERTY* (Mulla Mulla Press, 2011, Kalgoorlie). His novel *Blue Rose* is an enovel available through amazon.com and the publisher, eTextPress: http://www.etextpress.com/books.htm

Robbie COBURN was born in country Victoria, where he still resides. A writer of great diversity, he is currently working on a children's book and several screenplays and is also an actor and comedian. His first chapbook *Human Batteries* is set for release later this year, published by Picaro Press. Go to: www.robbiecoburn.com

Sophie CURZON-SIGGERS is 24 and a poet working in English and Italian, soon from a caravan in Victoria's Goldfields. She believes her late Netherlands Dwarf should be canonized for poetic miracles. Once aspired to shepherding, was briefly sought-after as a speaker on the pedagogical circuit, before finally yielding to the vocation of poetry.

Toby DAVIDSON is a West Australian poet, editor and reviewer now living in Sydney where he is an Australian Literature lecturer at Macquarie University. He is the editor of Francis Webb's *Collected Poems* (2011, ebook 2012) and author of the upcoming study *Born of Fire, Possessed by Darkness: Mysticism and Australian Poetry* (Cambria Press, 2013).

Matthew John DAVIES is a poet from Brisbane, Australia. He has been published in *Page Seventeen*, *Skive Magazine*, and *Rabbit*, as well as many journals both online and off.

Adrian FLAVELL lives and writes in the Adelaide Hills, SA. His poetry has appeared in a number of magazines, journals and newspapers in Australia and New Zealand. McGraw-Hill has published his series of three children's books *Dan's Days* in their Signature Series. The books are currently published by Clean Slate Press (NZ).

Aaron FURNELL is a power line construction worker from the remote West Coast of South Australia. A somewhat salacious soul tamed by the capitalist regime, he enjoys reading and writing, rap music and infrequent spells of binge drinking upon returning to the City of Churches.

Mike GREENACRE is a Western Australian poet who has had his poems published in literary journals and anthologies and read on radio in Australia and overseas. He is a teacher and has taught in The Kimberleys and The Goldfields before teaching in Perth schools in WA. He has published two collections of poetry: *Kimberley Man* (2002) and *Beacon Breaker* (2010). He is married to Tracy and they have a son Jonathan (24) and a daughter Jaime (22).

Yannis HONDROS lives in Perth, Western Australia, and currently teaches at Murdoch University. His poetry has appeared in a number of magazines and newspapers throughout Australia since the mid 70s. *Crossing Lines*, a volume of collected poems, was published in 2010. He has three sons and three grandchildren who fill in his life between punctuation marks.

Janet JACKSON writes poems, songs and prose, performs poetry and music, teaches poetry, helps organise Perth Poetry Club, parents and sometimes sleeps. Her publications include *Coracle* (2009), *q finger* (PressPress 2011), several zines, a micro-collection in Fremantle Press's forthcoming volume *Performance Poets* and her online collected works at *Proximity* (www.proximitypoetry.com).

Virginia JEALOUS' chapbook *Things Turned Upside Down* was released by Picaro Press in 2011. Virginia is a poet and travel writer, and in 2012 was awarded a three-month Asialink writing residency in India. She lives on the road and out of a suitcase when not at home in Denmark, Western Australia.

Peter JEFFERY (OAM) is heavily involved in Multicultural Art, Radio and Community Television and was recently Chair of WA Poetry Inc. He is returning to poetry after a long absence except for elegies for dear departed friends. He is hopeful of a collected verse anthology in the coming year.

Helga JERMY was born in the industrial midlands of England and migrated to Tasmania's rural north west coast 20 years ago, where she is employed as a social worker and writes short stories and poetry. Her work has been published online, including a recent *Australian Poetry* poem of the week, but this is her first contribution to a literary magazine.

Lorne JOHNSON lives in Bundanoon, NSW and teaches English at Magdalene Catholic High School in south-west Sydney. His poetry has appeared in *Meanjin, Island, Islet, Wet Ink, Mascara Literary Review, Eclogues* (The Newcastle Poetry Prize Anthology 2007), the Broadway Poetry Prize collection for 2004, *Your Times, Vegan Voice* and *Dogs Life*. He still regrets not seeing PiL live in '89. One day, he'll drive through the Deep South of the USA.

Amanda JOY is a poet, writer and installation artist, living in Fremantle Western Australia. Her work is concerned with poeticising temporality and invisible natural forces.

Rosalee KIELY has been published in *Voiceworks* and *dotdotdash*. She lives in Melbourne.

Christopher KONRAD lives and works in Perth. He has recently completed his PhD in creative writing and has had poems published with two other WA poets in a recent anthology called *Sandfire* (2012) and in many journals and on line. He works with the new and emerging communities.

Damon LOCKWOOD has been writing professionally for over ten years and has had his work produced all across the country. He won the national *Write Now!* 2005 competition for Best Script with his one-man show *Domestic Bliss* and his script *Pri-mates*, for Barking Gecko Theatre Company, was published in *The Australian Script Centre Collection #6*. *Nature as Explained by Theatre*, for Longwood Productions, was chosen as the *Play of the Month* for the Australian Script Centre. Other scripts include *Muttaburrasaurus* (Spare Parts Puppet Theatre), *Gogo Fish: The Fossil that Changed the World* (Barking Gecko Theatre Company), *12:15, Saturday Night* (Damage Theatre) and *A Change in the Weather*. Recent productions include *Horsehead, Short Four Play*, and *I (Honestly) Love*

You, all for Longwood Productions. Damon completed a year's mentorship with *Spare Parts Puppet Theatre* in 2005, and completed a co-production with *Deckchair Theatre Company* in October 2009 with two new scripts, *Forget-Me-Not* and *Refractions*. He has released a book of short stories with fellow West Aussie writer Nathan Hondros entitled *Man and Beast*. He currently holds the position of Artistic Associate with *Black Swan State Theatre Company*.

Harold MALLY lives Sydney and writes fiction. Some of his stories have appeared in publications such as *Blue Crow, Eclecticism, Narrator, Page Seventeen, Scribe, Splatter, 21D, [untitled]*, a couple of *Stringybark* publications and one made its way to the UK in *The Lighthouse Anthology*. A few have won awards. Many have done nothing at all.

Ari MATTES received his PhD from the University of Sydney in 2010, for a thesis tracing the development between classic American literature and action films. He has taught at Sydney University and ANU, and is currently lecturing in Australian literature at the University of Notre Dame, Sydney. He is a budding fiction writer, and is working on a novel as part of the MCA programme at UTS: a metaphysical thriller set in far North Queensland, Jim Thompson drenched in Faulkner. His story 'RomCom' appears in *Hide Your Fires*, the 2012 UTS Anthology.

Jan NAPIER work has been published in *Famous Reporter, Poetry New Zealand, dotdotdash, Unusual Work, Speed Poets, The Mozzie*, and other journals. Jan also writes book reviews for the online Sci Fi zine *Antipodean SF*.

Julia OSBORNE has been writing short stories for over 20 years. They have appeared in magazines and literary journals (notably *Meanjin, Island, Antipodes (USA)*, and anthologies. ABC Radio National has broadcast many of her short stories and one-act plays. She was awarded a Writer's Project Grant in 1991 for her novel *Falling Glass*, self-published in 2002 referencing the first Gulf War. Julia is now working on a young adult novella.

Chris PALAZZOLO is a novelist, poet and video store clerk who lives in Perth, Western Australia.

Kelly PILGRAM-BYRNE lives in Perth, Western Australia with her same-sex partner of 18 years and their four-year-old daughter. She has a BA Arts and a Postgraduate Diploma (Creative Writing) from Curtin University. Her poetry has been published in print and online journals. Her first collection of poetry, *People from bones* (with co-author, Bron Bateman) was released in the UK and Australia in June 2002 (publisher, Ragged Raven Press, UK). Her poem, 'Venus of Willendorf' was selected for the anthology, UQ's *Best Australian Poetry 2009*. Kelly's second collection, *Domestic Archaeology*, will be available from July 2012 through Grand Parade Poets. Centred on the universal themes of family life and on issues of fertility/infertility, her poems are public works of plain speaking vigour.

Rebecca RAISIN lives and writes in Perth. She's popular; the loves of her life all vie for her attention. Her twin boys are usually attached around each leg, which makes walking tricky, but doable. Her partner always wants to know what's for dinner, and insists everything is made from scratch. Her fictional friends beckon her to bed, where she spends far too much time…reading. The final draft of her first novel, *Mexican Kimono*, is almost finished. She tries to make everyone happy before opening up her laptop and killing people off.

Peter RONDEL — As a novice writer I attended Edith Cowan University at the age of sixty. Since then, I have had several stories and poems published in anthologies and children's poems in the *School Magazine*. My children's book *A Magpie Called Will* was published in America and is now on Amazon Books.

Zan ROSS is an American immigrant, living and breeding in Australia for over thirty years. She has been published in all the usual journals in this country as well as some in Budapest, Canada, France and the U.S. and featured in some online publications. She has two collections out, *B-Grade* through Monogene Press, and *Enpassant* through FACP, as well as the chapbook, *Je ne sais quoi* through Vagabond Press. She currently resides and occasionally works in Perth, WA.

Shey SAINT-MALO is a rehabilitated ex-scientist turned writer of poetry and fiction. Having recently completed a MA in Creative Writing, she got a haircut and a job in an attempt to shake off her professional student status, and can be found most days at the Katharine Susannah Prichard Writers' Centre.

Petri Ivalo SINDA's previous publications include a novelette in the inaugural volume of *Daikaiju!*, a cyberpunk story in the late online publication *Overland Express*, as well as a Mark Leyner-ish surreal comedy in *Paper Radio*. 'The Sound of Biological Functions' was inspired by a real-life anecdote related by Dr Karl on his weekly show for Triple J. Petri has recently relocated to Melbourne where he hopes to die of cappuccino poisoning.

Barnaby SMITH is a writer, journalist and editor based in Sydney's Inner West. After a childhood in the rural Hawkesbury, he lived in Europe for many years before returning to Australia in 2010. His poetry has appeared in *Southerly* and *Wet Ink* in 2012, while he also writes for *Rolling Stone*, *The Big Issue* and *The Quietus*.

Flora SMITH was a writer of short stories, magazine articles, and even a small history book before she began writing poetry eight years ago. She has been widely published in journals and anthologies around Australia, including *Westerly, indigo* and *Famous Reporter*. She writes mainly about people; their failings, hopes and dreams. Her curiosity about people came in part from her study and teaching of foreign languages, and from a great love of travel, which she finds a rich source of material for her poetry. She reads her work in various venues in Perth and Fremantle, and believes in actively serving the Perth poetry community.

Ian C. SMITH lives in the Gippsland Lakes region of Victoria. His work has appeared in *Axon:Creative Explorations*, *The Best Australian Poetry*, *Five Poetry Journal, Island, Red Room Company, Southerly* and *Westerly*. His fifth book is titled *Contains Language*, Ginninderra Press, Adelaide, 2011.

Kailash SRINIVASAN holds a Masters in Writing from Macquarie University, Sydney. He published his first book, *What Happened to That Love*, a short story collection, in 2010. His second book will be released by Gyaana Books in 2012. He's also part of a literary anthology to be published by O&S Publishing (Australia). Apart from this, some of his work has appeared in *Urban Shots – Love Collection, Bluslate Magazine*, and *Chicken Soup Books*.

Debbie STEPHAN is a writer of short stories and poetry and has worked as a local historian, publishing both pamphlets and books.

Ruth STUBBINGS is an experienced writer with a Bachelor's Degree in English Literature and a Master's Degree in Creative Writing. Her poetry has been published in student anthologies and various poetry prizes, but her true passion is in film writing. She is now working on several feature film scripts and has also been providing an editing and mentoring service to local unpublished writers and film students.

Gail WILLEMS is a semi-retired nurse, who writes when she can; in between living, swimming, and learning to surf and read Egyptian Hieroglyphs, which is not going so well. She has written two detective/narrative poems, is member of OOTA, has published online, in Belgium, New Zealand and Australia, on radio, in journals, magazines, anthologies and newspapers.

Warrick WYNNE is a Melbourne writer and teacher with three books of poetry, the most recent being *The State of the Rivers and Streams* (Five Islands). His home page is at www.warrickwynne.org.

www.ingramcontent.com/pod-product-compliance
Lightning Source LLC
Chambersburg PA
CBHW020647250626
47154CB00008B/2849